Complete Guide to Skip Tracing: The Art of Locating Missing Debtors

Thomas Stelter

Professional Education Systems, Inc.
P.O. Box 1208
200 Spring Street
Eau Claire, Wisconsin 54702
1-800-826-7155

ISBN 0-941161-16-1

The author of this publication is a professional in the field of skip tracing. The practices and techniques referred to within reflect effective and commonly used methods in the collection field. Certain of these techniques, which involve misrepresentation on the part of the professional and his or her associates, may be deemed as unethical by some. Please note that Professional Education Systems, Inc. neither advocates nor discourages these methods.

AUTHOR

THOMAS STELTER became aware of the need for this unique publication through his direct involvement in credit collection; he has managed and owned collection agencies throughout the United States for twenty-five years. He has received national recognition for his ability to locate credit skips, missing persons and lost heirs, and to complete difficult services of legal process. Mr. Stelter is the author of *SCAMS*, a training manual for credit granters, collection managers and repossessors of collateral and the *Lawyers' and Creditors' Service Directory*, the nation's most complete 1100-page forwarder's directory. He conducts numerous training seminars throughout the Midwest and is a much sought-after speaker at credit association conferences and seminars.

THE COMPLETE GUIDE TO SKIP TRACING: THE ART OF LOCATING MISSING DEBTORS

Table of Contents

Page

By Thomas Stelter

PREFACE

THE SEARCH "BETWEEN THE LINES"

If you have read *SCAMS*, you will know that I am very serious about my profession. I will go to any end to locate a skip or missing person. I hope that you are serious, too. This manual is not for anyone who practices the profession for less gratification than myself. The whole purpose of my writing this is to communicate with those persons out there who are sincere about this profession and want to know all that is possible to know about it. Even after all of the years that I have been locating people, I am still learning how. Times change, people change. Around every corner I find a new challenge facing me. Each and every skip is, in some way, different. We fail to find a skip because we only know how to make the usual inquiries. We do not utilize the imagination and thinking skills we have been given naturally. We do not read "between the lines."

Can you look into the mind of Lee Harvey Oswald and understand why he had to assassinate a president? Absolutely not! He did not fill out an *application*. If he had, however, the dastardly deed would have been prevented. We cannot look into the minds of those who skip away on us and know why they left or where they have gone. But we do have one important advantage: WE HAVE AN APPLICATION, I HOPE! With this, we are much more able to look into the mind of the subject and understand why he had to skip and maybe even where he went. With this tool, we have the direction in front of us, and our job becomes more general, more procedural. This is what we have learned to do so far in our skills. I am not saying that your job has been an easy one, by any means. If you have gotten this far, to wanting to read this manual, you have already had enough experiences to make you feel confident in this profession. I hope that this book will bring you even more exciting and new experiences. The deeper that you get BETWEEN THE LINES, the more rewarding your experience is going to be. The deeper that you have to go, or feel a need to go, the more you will begin to understand.

In *SCAMS*, I tried to relay to the reader how important an accurate application is. I indicated that it is not so much what the applicant said about himself that is important as that which he avoided saying. Therefore, if we don't have a credit manager who is as skilled as we are, we may be facing a tough road whenever one of HIS debtors skips. However, even the worst credit application can give you the building blocks you need to develop the clues you need to find your skip.

In the very beginning of my career, which started as a field collector, I realized that there was a lesson to be learned in every account I had to collect. Each and every debtor had a new reason why he could not pay on his account. "It's in the mail" became old stuff. I had to learn to outwit these people — all during a time when consumer advocates were saying that I was not able to do the things I was doing and/or say the things that I was saying. Each day was a new idea. Every collection was a new scam. My job was to collect on the accounts six or more months overdue. Among these were the skips. As a field collector, I had the advantage of being in their town, where most of their history usually was. A few select questions here and there usually brought the right answers, and I would find the skip.

Collection is no more than a communications effort. But, to communicate means that you must know where the debtor is. In every case, to collect we need a listener. I hope that within the following pages of this manual, I have found those listeners that desire to know as much as they can about skip tracing and that they will gain some new information that will make them better skip tracers. That will be my reward.

IN THE BEGINNING

Although a professional skip tracer deals with matters of all sorts, with and without the advantage of an application, I have decided to structure the beginning of this manual using one of the toughest credit applications that I have ever seen. To say the least, this application has guts. Or the person who conceived it did. But, remember this: The legitimate credit seeker who has every honest intention to repay his lender would never object to filling out such an application. Those that do object are the ones that you should take a closer look at. If I had had my way during my many years as a credit grantor and collector, I would have liked to use this application in every case I had. I have not found a credit grantor who would be willing to use such an application. They have always been to eager to build their receivables and felt that this application would scare potential customers away. Today's concept of easy credit has virtually doomed many businesses to failure. Poor credit acceptance criteria are giving the advantage to the debtors. Debtors are now educated! You have to be on your toes every time your application is filled out. They are so good that they can beat you *too* often.

Because skip tracers have to follow up on the acts of those credit grantors, it is valuable that we know how to assimilate the information (good or bad) that we have been given to work with and find our skips. The application is broken down into several parts:

PERSONAL INFORMATION

JOB INFORMATION

CREDIT INFORMATION

REFERENCE INFORMATION.

Each part must be analyzed carefully for

IDENTITY

HONESTY

ACCURACY.

We not only have to look at and analyze the things we are told, but we have to discern and interpret the things that we are not told. We must be able to READ BETWEEN THE LINES! If, by some chance, you are thinking to yourself that this is tough, think about those cases you will face without an application to work from. How about the day that your client calls you and tells you how desperate he is to talk to an important witness and tells you that his name is John Smith, AND THAT IS ALL HE KNOWS! How are you going to handle that?

I recall the first time that I was faced with a name-only case. In 1974, I was asked to locate a witness to a stabbing on a city bus. I was given this man's name only. After hours of contemplation, having used up all of the usual resources, I found myself in dead city. Rather than confuse myself any further, I sat back and pondered on the information that I did have. That did not take long. I then reread the police report, looking for new clues. An idea came alive!

The stabbing had happened at 3:10 p.m. on a crowded bus. The bus had been southbound on 27th Street and stopped at the Wisconsin Avenue crossing after the stabbing took place. WHY NOT? That afternoon, at the same time, I waited on the corner until the bus arrived. Since city buses arrive at each stop at designated times, I was confident that I would get on the very same bus. The police report stated that the witness had been on the bus at the time of the stabbing, which occurred before the bus reached the corner. I was not interested in the people who were waiting with me. The bus arrived and I let all of the other people get on first so as not to interfere with the driver's duties. When I got on, I identified myself to the driver and told him why I was there.

He allowed me to address the people on the bus. Believe this! Not only was my subject on the bus, but two other people who had witnessed the stabbing gave me their names and addresses. Needless to say, my client was very happy.

Reading between the lines, even with such little information, gave me the idea I needed to resolve this case. And, this is what you will have to learn to practice.

THE APPLICATION

PERSONAL INFORMATION

1-NAME | 2-MAIDEN OR NICK-NAME | 3-AGE | 4-PHONE

5-PERSON LIVING WITH YOU | 6-MAIDEN OR NICK-NAME | 7-AGE | 8-RELATIONSHIP | 9-NAME PHONE IS IN

10-ADDRESS | 11-APARTMENT NO. | 12-CITY | 13-ZIP CODE | 14-COUNTY

15-LANDLORD'S NAME | 16-ADDRESS | 17-PHONE

18-HOW LONG AT THIS ADDRESS | 19-HOW LONG IN THIS CITY | 20-IF MARRIED, HOW LONG

21-PREVIOUS ADDRESS | HOW LONG THERE

EMPLOYMENT INFORMATION

22-EMPLOYED BY | 23-ADDRESS | 24-PHONE

25-OCCUPATION | 26-HOW LONG | 27-DEPARTMENT | 28-SUPERVISOR'S NAME

29-WORKING HOURS From | To | 30-PAY DAY | 31-SALARY $

32-PREVIOUS EMPLOYER | 33-HOW-LONG | 34-PHONE

35-EMPLOYER OF PERSON LIVING WITH YOU | 36-ADDRESS | 37-PHONE

38-OCCUPATION | 39-HOW LONG | 40-DEPARTMENT | 41-SUPERVISOR'S NAME

42-WORKING HOURS From | To | 43-PAY DAY | 44-SALARY $

45-PREVIOUS EMPLOYER | 46-HOW LONG | 47-PHONE

48-WELFARE/OTHER INCOME $ | 49-CASE NO. | 50-CASE WORKER'S NAME | 51-PHONE | 52-PAY DATES | 53-AMOUNT $

54-WHAT IS YOUR HOME TOWN? | 55-NAME/ADDRESS/PHONE OF CONTACT PERSON THERE

56-SOCIAL SECURITY NO. | 57-BIRTH DATE | 58-DRIVER'S LICENSE NO. | HEIGHT | WEIGHT | EYES | HAIR

59-SOCIAL SECURITY NO. | 60-BIRTH DATE | 61-DRIVER'S LICENSE NO. | HEIGHT | WEIGHT | EYES | HAIR

62-NAME | 63-AGE | 64-GRADE | 65-SCHOOL

NAME | AGE | GRADE | SCHOOL

NAME | AGE | GRADE | SCHOOL

NAME | AGE | GRADE | SCHOOL

66-RENTER'S INSURANCE

67-BANK NAME | 68-BRANCH ADDRESS | 69-☐ Checking ☐ Savings

70- NAME UTILITIES ARE IN

71-YEAR AND MODEL OF CAR | 72-COLOR | 73-LICENSE PLATE NO. | 74-STATE

PERSONAL REFERENCES — Relatives, Friends, Neighbors

75-Name	76-Address	77-Relationship	78-Home Phone Number

CHILDREN

I have numbered the blank, fill-in spaces in the preceding application, and we will look at the value of each. Remember, each time you take apart any of these items, you may develop any number of leads that may take you in any number of directions. Your depth of concentration, your imagination, and your desire to resolve will guide your will to win, no matter how tough the skip is. Whether it be a lot or just a little information, you have to work it anyway.

CHAPTER ONE
PERSONAL INFORMATION

ITEM #1 WHAT IS THERE IN A NAME?

A name can tell you a lot if you know what to look for. It can give you a nationality, a religion, an ethnic area, or even an ethnic association. The obvious direction, however, is to make sure that you have the correct name and spelling. Do you have the full name? I want to remind you now that we are getting into skip tracing in an analytical sense and that you should have already worked your skip through the general skip trace procedure. Even if you think that the name of your subject is spelled correctly, you should make an effort to make very sure. Even a common name like Smith can be mistaken for Smyth, Smythe, Schmid, or even Schmidt. Making sure can save you many hours of fruitless work should you be wrong. I can give you a good example of this.

I had a missing heir case several years ago, and the name I was provided with was misspelled. I ignored my own rules and proceeded to search for an individual with the last name of Ambur. I worked on this matter for three days and became frustrated because I could not find that last name listed anywhere. I had checked several states, including the eastern states, as the basic origination of most names is from that area. The last known address provided was a hotel, and I recognized it from the start. Now, who would think that a hotel would have records over eleven years old? You're right. They didn't, either. However, I was informed that this hotel had converted several floors to permanent apartments for elderly persons. They still had no record of this individual. I resorted once again to my collection of city directories and began a year-by-year search of the hotel address. I was still going back, year by year, when in the 1959 edition of the *Wright's Directory*, I found a name very similar to the Ambur name. I called back to the hotel and spoke to the lady who had kept the records of the apartments. Yes! She did remember this lady and her husband, too. She provided me with the name of the party's attorney. Just one phone call resolved the case, and I earned $3,400.00 commission. You can see now why you must be sure that you have a correct name to work with. Would you have gone this far?

When working Item #1, the first area of your search is in the telephone directories in the subject's last area and also in the surrounding areas. You are looking for same last names at the same last known address (wife, brother, sister, cousin, mother, father), same last names in the same area (twenty surrounding city blocks), and same last names anywhere in the city or surrounding towns.

When calling these people, you should assume that they know of your subject and how you may be able to reach him. Therefore, when your call is answered, ask for your subject by his name as though you think he is at that phone. Stick with this procedure until you find someone who thinks or says that he knows the person you are calling about. Get all of the information you can about the person he knows — for example, parents or other relatives who may know how you can contact your subject. See if he knows if the person he is thinking of lived at the address you have or at any previous address you know of. If you have a record of where your subject was employed or the type of profession he was in, see if your source has knowledge that compares with yours. When gathering any information of this sort, make sure that you ask for the location of the individuals your source is mentioning to you and possibly their phone numbers. You never know who has a nonpublished phone number. Derive a scam to use in the event that someone wants to know why you are looking for this subject. Make it a reason important enough that people will feel the need to give you the information freely. Gathering information this way will usually resolve your case if your subject is originally from the area. Yet, in these modern times, families seem to split apart and quite often have very little contact. Always be ready and well practiced with your scams. Stumble and you will no longer be able to ask any further questions. Keep your notes, even if you have not found out anything that you feel is important. What you have may become important later. Follow up on those callbacks and no-answers. Do not leave any stones unturned. Reread your notes after this procedure and after every procedure that you take. You often will see things that you missed the first time.

Take the name through a check of the local utilities. If you have not made contacts in these areas yet, I suggest that you do so as soon as you can. Take the name through a check of the local public record areas: welfare, unemployment, police files, probation and parole, court files — civil and divorce. The above are public record in many areas of the country but are still held confidential in others. Try to develop contacts in these areas also. The above can provide you with the following information:

Welfare

Note: In almost all areas, the records of unwed mothers and Aid to Dependent Children cases are still held confidential. A check of the welfare rolls can provide you with a possible new address, the name of a relative, job-training programs your subject may have gone through or is currently going through, the name of the individual's case worker, the name of the school that the children attend. When speaking to case workers, you will find that they are usually very protective of their clients. You might find it advantageous to become familiar with your state statutes on public records and the obligations of the record holders. Do not hesitate to remind or quote the statutes when trying to obtain information. If they still resist your request for information, contact the administrative offices. I have found that developing a contact within a welfare fraud unit has simplified these requests. To do their jobs and look good, these people are grateful for any information you may give them regarding any welfare fraud matter you may stumble onto. And as a professional skip tracer, you will run across some.

Unemployment Compensation Records

As a matter of public interest, these records are available only because the fund for unemployment benefits comes from the employers. As an employer interested in giving the subject work, you have the right to any information regarding the unemployment record of your subject. Naturally, you will inquire as to the address that the subject's compensation checks are being sent to. Here again, overzealous employees of this unit may believe that these records are held confidential. Although it may vary from one state to another, I am sure that you can find a method within the law by which to obtain them. For example, the employer who is currently paying on the compensation is being provided with the address that the checks are being sent to on the forms it receives. You might contact that employer. It may be contesting the claim, and a hearing may be forthcoming. You might want to attend that hearing or call the clerk who schedules them. He will also have the subject's current address.

Police Files

These are the hardest of all records to obtain. The hassle for these records in large cities makes the attempt time consuming and usually fruitless. The quickest way to these records is to seek out a FRIEND or make a friend who is on the force. If you cannot arrange this kind of source, you will have to search your individual state's statutes or contact the public information officer in your police department. The computers there store information concerning the subject's police-related history, including the most recent traffic stops and checks they may have made.

Smaller communities offer less resistance when asked for these records. Quite often, they are interested in your reason for inquiring for their own knowledge, and you may find them cooperative.

Probation and Parole

Each community keeps records of commitments, misdemeanors, and felonies. You have the right as a citizen to inspect these records. The state maintains records of all commitments within the state. These are also available; however, you are generally asked to make your request in writing. It is usually quicker if you know what community a commitment was issued in. A phone call to the records room will usually gain information about any current or previous commitments and the name of the probation or parole officer assigned to the subject. You even may find that your subject is currently residing in some jail awaiting trial or has already been sentenced to an institution. The term of the sentence, the crime, and the release date are public record.

The federal government also has a public records office concerning persons placed on probation and parole and those incarcerated. Federally controlled persons have the right to move from state to state, but there are guidelines which provide that they must ask permission and are assigned a new agent in the area that they are moving to. The authorities in that area also require that they be notified.

An individual that has been placed on probation or is out on parole is assigned a case worker. It is the duty of this worker to make sure that his ward is living a responsible and lawful life within the community. Therefore, the agent should have no objection to giving you the latest address or work information on your subject. He may even appreciate knowing that he does not have a current address on his ward and that his ward may be skipping him also. In his records, he has information about the ward's family, etc. He also has instant access to any police records, and you very well may be able to recruit his aid.

Court Files — Civil and Divorce

A check of the court files in both areas may render to you a bag of information concerning your subject. The most valuable, of course, would be an address at which your subject recently was served legal papers. Other information would be names of creditors and lawyers, whether there is a divorce pending, and the address of the spouse.

I mentioned earlier that a name can suggest a number of things to you. Again, I want to remind you that many times you are going to have to go to extreme measures to develop a lead. The ethnic areas of a city are, for the most part, still segregated. It is usually by personal choice that one seeks out his own kind. Therefore, you should concentrate your efforts within these areas unless you already know that your subject has broken out of these confines. A select few of every race do not wish to be stereotyped within a specific ethnic area and make the break. These few are by far the hardest to locate because they are willing to go anywhere.

If religion can be entered into our search, as the Irish are known to be predominantly Catholic, other races are also associated with certain religions. If you are not able to establish any specific religious ties, you may want to call around to the churches in the subject's last known area. Many times, a pastor of one of these churches has worked hard to bring your subject's family into his fold and may have information about him. You may even find yourself talking to his minister. Smaller communities offer a better opportunity for your inquiries as there are fewer churches. Your subject may have belonged to one of them, or a minister may know the subject or at least other members of the family.

Grocery stores and service stations in the last known area are also within those last-ditch areas. I say "last-ditch" because you have other items to search from this application and should really reserve these areas as desperate moves. However, a grocer can possibly tell you where your subject worked or did his banking if he had check-cashing privileges at the store. He may have gotten to know him well enough to tell you the names of some of his friends. The service station owner may also have information for you if the subject regularly brought his car in for service. Service station owners are often more friendly than grocers in larger cities. This is not true for small communities. Anybody could know everything about anybody in a small town. I have, over the years, called co-ops, grocers, service stations, restaurants, and bars in small towns and resolved cases just on those calls alone. I have taken just about any name out of a small-town telephone directory and called it and gotten a wealth of information concerning my subject. Other areas in which you can search out your subject's name are tavern sports leagues, pool leagues, and bowling leagues.

Dads like to name sons after themselves. However, nobody really likes to be called "Junior." The more recent trend is to name a child with the father's middle name or give a child a name using the same initials as Dad's. Therefore, W.L. Grant in your phone book may be the father of your subject, William Lawrence Grant. Or, Jon A. Wilton may be the father of John A. Wilton. William T. Mear was the father of T. William Mear in one of my cases. Once, while looking for Lorraine (last name deleted), I spent numerous hours searching for a lady who never existed. The Lorraine I was searching for turned out to be a man. My younger brother and I both named our sons Richard after our father. I gave my youngest son the middle name of Thomas, as in my first name. So you see, there can be valuable information in a name.

ITEM #2 MAIDEN NAME OR NICKNAME

Next to the wife's mother as a source of information, a maiden name is the second most valuable skip trace tool you may have. Where a nickname only comes into play with friends and sports activities, a maiden name can open a whole new set of doors. For example, with regard to nicknames, several years ago I was contacted by an attorney regarding an assault that took place on one of his clients in a tavern. It seemed that his client had been mistaken for another person and was terribly beaten by an individual known only as "Magoo." The attorney wanted me to identify and locate this Magoo character so that he could name him as the principal defendant in a lawsuit along with the bar owner and insurance carrier. The attorney had already contacted the bar owner and was told that he did not know who Magoo was. It was his feeling that the bar owner was not telling the truth.

In many instances, a nickname is descriptive of an individual's character, habits, name, or physical make-up. "Ski" is a derivative of a Polish name. "Leggs" is a dancer or a runner. "Mighty Mouse" is a body builder or a weight lifter, and "Specs" is someone who wears thick glasses. To me, "Magoo" fit in the character of "Specs." I learned that you cannot always characterize a nickname.

On the second night of my surveillance, I was sitting at the bar in question when three salty-looking characters walked in. The bar owner, who was tending the bar, called the three men over to him and, referring to the trouble they had caused on a prior occasion, asked them to leave and stay away for awhile. The apparent leader of the trio began arguing with the owner. The owner then referred to him by saying,

"Magoo, you are going to get me in a lot of trouble." I knew I had found my man. Now all I had to do was identify him by who he really was. I left the tavern while they were still arguing so that I would not have to follow them out. I found a walkway a few buildings away from the tavern and waited. When they came out, I observed them walking down the street and going into another tavern. I looked into the window of this tavern, and they were served without any trouble. I decided to sit in my car, which was down the block, and wait for them to leave. Almost three hours later, they came out and walked away from me. Just as I was about to start my car, they crossed the street and climbed into a car. As they went by me, I got the license plate number. Magoo was driving. The next morning I ran the license number and got the full name, address, and such. To this day I wonder why this man was referred to as "Magoo."

A son can go on with his life away from his family and never communicate with them. Even if he does, he rarely tells his family very much other than "I'm fine. Don't worry." A daughter, however, almost always stays in touch with her mother. I must say here that getting information from her mom will not be an easy task. Moms are naturally very protective of their daughters. Your story had better be straight and contain accurate facts. When talking to a mother-in-law, I prefer asking questions about her son-in-law. A mother-in-law usually carries a seemingly natural suspicious attitude about her daughter's husband, the guy who took her little girl away, and usually is willing to talk about him in an effort to know if he is treating her daughter right. Arouse her ire about him, and you may get more answers than you bargained for. I do not mean here that you should try to belittle him. Rather, make your inquiry as though it would be to *his* advantage if you were able to contact him. You must first make her trust you. Play around with several pitches until you are confident that you have one that gets a relaxed response.

As we do not always have an application to work with, we sometimes have to work very hard to find out who the wife's parents are. Several ways of finding out the wife's maiden name that I find quick and accessable are marriage records, credit bureau records, employers, driver's license records, neighbors, references, medical records, and welfare records.

Once you have obtained her maiden name and you still have no other information about her whereabouts, you can go back to Item #1 of this chapter. Another point that I would like to bring up at this time is that before you attempt to skip trace any case, you should review your material to see if you have any source from which you may pick up a copy of an application made by your subject or get information from an application. We make applications for many things other than credit. We make rental applications, job applications, membership applications, and many others. If you think you have a lead to such information, follow it. The application source can be part of your basic skip trace effort if you do not have any direction in the very beginning. Once you have uncovered an old job or an old address, you may still be able to get information from that source. When you have come to a dead end in trying to search for current information on your subject, you can always go backward. Many times, this is the best way to begin your search.

An insurance company contacted me recently concerning the location of a beneficiary. Locating a beneficiary is by far the hardest kind of case you can have. In almost all cases, you start with a name-only situation. Your case can be compounded in difficulty several times over if the party you are seeking is a nonfamily member. As was the case here, my subject was a friend of long standing. In fact, as it turned out, he had come to this country on the same boat with the deceased. At first I thought that I was facing a hard locate, but after reviewing the information I had been given, I noted that the insurance policy had originated through the deceased man's job. I contacted the employer, which was still in the newspaper business. Sure enough, it had maintained the employment records of the deceased even though he had retired years before. The employer told me that he had worked for its ethnic newspaper for all of the years that he was in America until he retired. Although no one there knew the beneficiary, they did now that his best friend was also his neighbor and lived in the house next to where he had lived. Hopeful that I had come close to resolving this case, I called the public library in Baltimore and had the reference clerk search back in the city directories until we discovered that the subject beneficiary and the address had been removed from the directory several years before the insured passed away. I could find no current information on the subject. I then contacted the city of Baltimore records clerk and found out that the subject had in fact died before the insured. I checked out the subject's probate file while I was checking out the same file for the insured. Neither of them had any relatives in attendance during probate. In fact, the court had assigned a local attorney to represent each of them. There were no heirs in either case, and all funds had since escheated to the state. Having received no authority to go further, I reported my findings to my client, and that was the last I heard of that matter.

Therefore, it is usually necessary to go into the past for clues. A maiden name will give you other things to look for besides the parents.

Of course, brothers or unmarried sisters, if there are any, may still be around. Your clues are more often made by your work than handed to you.

ITEM #3 AGE

Age can also say something to you. Let's say that our subject is in his early twenties and recently married (within five years or so). Most marriages that fall apart disintegrate during those first years. Overextension of credit and the problems it brings a young married couple can quickly create an attitude of insecurity that often leads to breakup and divorce. This situation, as we know, does exist in all age groups but is much more prevalent in the first few years of marriage.

We live our lives in age cycles so to speak: youth, teens, young adulthood, adulthood, middle age, and old age. Each of these areas in our lives can dictate our habits. Between the ages of twenty-five and forty, we are restless animals. If we have not been successful in our jobs or professions, we continue searching for those new areas which will bring us stability and satisfaction. Many of the people that have this attitude will never find what they think they are looking for because they really have no idea what it is. The truth is that although, time after time, opportunities were before them, they either didn't recognize them or were not willing to work for them. And what is the consequence of this? They always believe that they will be able to make it better with a fresh start. So, to have this new start without being impeded by old creditors, they slink away to different areas. In their minds, they think that their intentions are good. They believe that if they can keep creditors off their backs for a while, they can make it all different and will contact those creditors later. Don't bet on it! They are waiting for your next move. They will wait forever if you let them!

After the fortieth birthday, we find a whole new set of circumstances. Creditors become too comfortable with those who have always been thought of as good, sound credit risks and allow them almost unharnessed credit privileges. A great number of very financially sound people have suddenly found themselves in bad financial condition because they planned poorly or not at all for illness. I think that people in this age category suffer the most from a sudden change of circumstances because they are usually more soundly settled and satisfied that they have established themselves in their lives. Having already gone through most of the hard times in life (in a credit sense), they have the very unique ability to hide themselves. By this time their parents have passed away, and their brothers and sisters have spread around the country. There is now very little in sight to aid you in locating them.

Your first area to search would be the financial area. Hopefully, your subject has tried to maintain a rapport with at least one of his favorite creditors or has tried to re-establish one with one of his paid-up creditors. His credit cards become even more valuable to him at this time because he is travelling with very limited cash. He knows that the credit card companies will not start any collection activity until he is sixty or ninety days past due. If you are able to communicate with those creditors, they may be interested to know that you are chasing him for other creditors and may cooperate with you in your search.

I have never promised to let other creditors know where the subject is and then not done so when I found him. To do this would be a disaster to your reputation. Anyway, the game of skip tracing and your ability lay strongly in the stability of the inside contacts you have made. Don't mess any of them up and always let your contact know that you will be glad to help him anytime. See if you can get him to arrange other contacts within his organization. He may leave and go on to better things someday.

Now, for those wonderful people over the age of sixty. They have worked hard for many years with the hope that at this age they could relax in some comfort. Barring financial disasters due to illnesses, many of them are able to retire and enjoy their later years.

A deadbeat at sixty? Absolutely! Another recent case of mine is a prime example. With over forty years on the same job, the subject had always had a livable income and no debt to pay to anyone. However, this man now had only his retirement check and Social Security to live on. Well, anyway, it was time to have some fun — just to be able to relax and enjoy. How about some credit cards? He had never had one and had always paid cash. Well, just a few, O.K.? Two gas cards and a VISA card. With these in his pocket, he could take his wife and himself on trips that they had always only dreamed about, and he would not have to carry a lot of cash. The car was pretty old, so he made a good deal on a truck-camper and financed it. So far, he was still within his ability to make the payments.

The very first trip was a disaster. The engine overheated and they threw a rod. It took all of his available cash and one of his gas credit cards to buy a junk-yard engine and have it installed. He didn't mean to harm or cheat anyone, but now he was behind in all of his credit payments. Confused and unable to think out this crisis, he continued to travel around the country on the credit cards until they were cancelled. His retirement and Social Security checks were being automatically deposited into his checking account, and he was somewhere in the state of Colorado when he found out that his VISA card was no longer valid. Upon calling the bank to find out why, he was informed that his account had been garnisheed by the lien holder of his truck-camper and that he could no longer use his VISA card. He and his wife moved into a small, low-rent cottage in Arvada, Colorado, and contacted his union and the Department of Social Security to have his checks sent to him there. All went well for awhile. He even found a job as a janitor at a private school.

I was not aware of the circumstances of this case at the time I was hired to locate him. I did so and made arrangements for a repossession of the truck-camper. Sure, when I had all of the facts of this matter, I felt bad, as anyone would. But, this is my profession. I am supposed to be immune to such feelings.

ITEM #4 THE TELEPHONE

In every major city, there are always certain prefixes (the first three numbers) that are reserved for pay telephones. This is also true for non-published numbers. You should try to familiarize yourself with these prefixes. I believe that there are three kinds of nonpublished numbers available: unpublished (that for which no information is available); unlisted address (where no address is printed in the directory); and unlisted (where no phone number or address is printed and can only be obtained by calling information). The prefix of a telephone number will usually imply a certain area of a city. If you are able to establish that area, it could shorten your work time. Before we go further, however, we must determine what the number will tell us.

Was this number, or is this number, still listed to the subject? You can determine this by looking in the phone book, calling information, checking the cross-index directories that are available in your area, or just by calling the number. "Hello, repair service here. We have had a report of trouble on this line. Can you hold up your receiver while I perform a line test? (PAUSE) I think that there is a malfunction in your instrument. I would like to send someone out to check it. What address are you at, and if there is an apartment number, I'll need that, too. So I can pull our record, what name is this phone listed to?" This simple pitch or variations of it work for me almost all of the time.

If the number you have been given is not listed to your subject, who is it listed to? You may find one of several things. He was using an alias. He had it listed in the name of a friend or relative. He used the name of one of his children. It was listed under the wife's maiden name, her brother, her sister, or other. Any one of these names could be a clue for you. Many times, I have had to locate a friend or a relative in order to even start a skip trace procedure — a sort of double skip! Many times, also, I have found that where the phone was listed to a roommate, I could find the roommate, and gain more knowledge about the subject.

Do you have a contact at the telephone company? If you do, protect it by all means. Of all sources, this one has always been the hardest one to maintain. Security is a priority matter with telephone companies. I had to learn the hard way, many years ago, that developing a source in this area is difficult. It seems that the telephone company offers incentive rewards to its employees not only for money-saving ideas, but also for disclosure of security leaks. If employees are approached by anyone, they are enticed by rewards to contact their security department. In the opposite, they face termination of employment without appeal if they are caught giving out information.

I mentioned that I learned the hard way. Actually, it was not hard on me but on the information operator who was supplying me with addresses for people with nonpublished phones. Every day, during her morning break, she would call me and I would give her a list of names. She would call me back during her afternoon break and give me all of the addresses. Apparently she told a fellow operator about this arrangement, and the other girl contacted security. Her termination came one day only moments after she had called me in the afternoon to give me the information. I had cautioned her not to tell anyone about our deal. At ten dollars for each address, she was making more money from me than she was being paid by the telephone company. I had lost a valuable source, and it took me several months to replace her.

Sometimes, when you are dealing with a skip that is several months old or more, you will find that the telephone, even though it is listed to your subject in the phone book, is answered by a person who tells you that the number no longer belongs to your subject. This could often be true. In larger metropolitan areas, because of a need for available numbers, the telephone companies will reassign a number as soon as within thirty days. They make a survey test on the number to see how many times it is being called, and when they are satisfied that not too many calls will come in to inconvenience the new subscriber, they assign the line. In spite of this survey, many times you will call these numbers and have to listen to some very upset people. Hard collection activity does not begin until an account is more than thirty days old, and you can imagine the number of calls that could be placed to a number that had been assigned to someone who skipped out on his creditors. It is most amazing to know how many collectors are not aware of this and harass these people anyway. It is a simple matter to confirm this reassignment by calling information to see if your subject has a phone listed at any address.

I determined once that a number was listed to a lady whose name gave no obvious relationship to my subject. Thinking that I might have reached a reassigned number, I was about to take my search in other areas when I noted that this lady had been more upset than agitated by my call. In fact, her response was more practiced than usual. I decided to check further. The first thing that I found by checking the old phone books, year by year, was that this telephone had been listed to the same lady for a great number of years. My collection of telephone directories goes back about fifteen years, and she appeared in a phone book about seven years old with the same name at a different address — THE ADDRESS THAT MY SUBJECT HAD SKIPPED FROM! Further investigation indicated that this woman was not only the property owner of the skip's address, but she was the mother of the skip — remarried, name changed, and renting her home to her daughter. The telephone listing at that address was listed to the mother's previous name, which was also unlike her daughter's. I checked the current directory and found that this number had still been listed to the address at the last printing. I called the number, and an intercept operator (now know as a computer) told me that the number had been changed and gave me the new number. I called information and asked for a listing and an address for this name. I was given both, and the number matched. I had found the skip!

The status of a telephone number can indicate to you any of several conditions:

BUSY SIGNAL (Sixty per minute) — The phone is busy or may be off the hook. You will receive the same signal if someone else is ringing the phone at the same time you are.
BUSY SIGNAL (120 per minute) — The trunk lines are busy. Continue to replace your call.
TEMPORARILY DISCONNECTED — This report could mean one of two things. He is moving to a new residence within the same prefix area and wants to keep the same number, or he is very delinquent on his bill and the phone company has discontinued his service until he pays up.
DISCONNECTED — He did not pay his bill, or he had the phone disconnected.
PHONE NUMBER WAS CHANGED TO UNPUBLISHED — This may or may not indicate that your subject has moved. Sometimes they do this to give themselves a breather from their creditors. More often, though, when a deadbeat skips and stays in the same area and does not know how to hide, he will have his service installed unpublished.

To determine if a listing is in the name of your subject, you need only call your information operator. The operator cannot give you or confirm an unlisted number but must confirm the identity of your subject by acknowledging that the address you have is the same as his.

An unpublished number on a credit application usually indicates that a debtor has had problems or is still having problems with another creditor. There are several reasons that legitimate people do have non-published phone service — policemen, judges, public officials. Some business and service business professionals have this service to avoid receiving unwanted calls at their homes. Collectors who use their real names also prefer this service.

As a skip tracer, your ability to evaluate a phone number is how you will be able to develop workable leads in this area. Oddly enough, just before I started this sentence, I was called by my secretary into the other room to assist her in a problem she was having. It seems that she had a phone number that was being answered every time she called. She was being told that the party she sought was not in town and would return at the beginning of next month. She had sent one of our field agents to the address at which the phone was listed and was told that there was no longer a business listed there in the name of the phone holder. This was strange to her because both the city cross-index and the information operator indicated that the number was still listed to that address. I called a law office at the same address and asked for the name of the new building owner (as I knew that this other party had owned the building). Upon calling the building owner, I found out that his office in the same building was answering the phone which had been moved upstairs. The subject person had moved to Florida over a year ago, and the new owner gave me the name of the subject's attorney, who was handling his local business.

No call forwarding was used in this matter. Rather, to hide himself from the many creditors trying to reach him, he took advantage of a friend who was now sick and tired of receiving all of these calls — to the point that he was now telling everyone where the man went and whom to contact.

Call Forwarding

This is a real devil! Until the telephone company gets around to disconnecting the subject's telephone, he can still receive his calls at a different address, where he probably has service in another name. Trying to field collect from the subject or serve legal papers on him becomes a real pain.

The solution to this condition is to train field people to ask questions of the neighbors whenever they go out on a call and find no one home. At least you will know that the subject is still in town, and you can direct your search in other areas. But, watch out! If the subject has no intention of paying his phone bill, he may be transferring those calls long distance. Do not be surprised if, when you contact a friend or relative, you are told that he has moved out of town.

Answering Machines

I hate them. Not only might you have just paid for a long-distance call, but the subject is now screening his calls and can decide if he wants to talk to you or not. You are going to have to be pretty witty to get him to call. Message tapes are usually only several minutes long. I like to fill them up with my message and return phone number until he gets mad enough to call me to complain. If he is nasty and unresponsive, you might try duplicating the message tone on his tape and repeatedly filling his tape with beeps.

Long-Distance Leads

Let's assume that you have finally gotten someone to give you your subject's phone number or a number where he can be reached in another city. The first thing I like to do is find out what city I am going to be searching in. As mentioned earlier, big cities and small towns call for different activities.

You are given the number 312-886-1074. If you do a lot of long-distance calling, you already know that this area code is in the northeast part of Illinois. Now, dial the operator and tell her, "Name place please for 312-886." She will provide you with the name of the city or the town in which the phone is listed. Now call information. If the number is not an unlisted one, you can get the new address from the operator. If it is an unlisted phone, you at least have established the area that the subject is in.

If you are told that this is a number of somewhere where he can be reached, you can call the Chamber of Commerce or the public library and have them search their city directory or *Polk's*, *Johnson's*, *Wright's* and other directories that list telephone numbers numerically. This will usually identify the owner of the number. Then, during the same call, you can have that name checked in the directory or local phone book for an address.

This number may turn out to be that of a business, and the skip may work there. I once had an operator tell me that "all calls to this number are being handled by another number." She gave me the number along with an area code. Upon calling that number, I found myself talking to a truck driver dispatcher who took messages for the subject. This dispatcher was able to tell me where the subject was at that time, where he was heading next, and when he was scheduled to arrive at home again. So, don't despair when you find a disconnected number.

There is one other item I would like to mention before closing this chapter. GARBAGE! Yes, even garbage is important to you. Toll sheets listing long-distance calls are rarely kept by people. They are usually thrown into the garbage. If you are lucky enough to get to a skip's garbage can before it is removed, you may gain a wealth of information. You may find numbers and area codes on the toll sheets that probably belong to relatives, friends, or potential employers. I have found numbers of stockbrokers, hospitals, and many other parties that were related in some way to the skip's direction of travel. One case I recall involved a number that led me to a Marine induction center in Chattanooga, Tennessee. Upon further inquiry, I found out that the skip had in fact joined the Marines and felt that he had to do so from his home town. Many other things can be found in the garbage can — doctors' names, names of other creditors, letters from friends and relatives, and magazine subscription notices.

One day, while searching for a skip for a major credit card company, I noticed on the charge slip that he had paid for a subscription to a trade magazine. I contacted the magazine mailing department in Des Moines, Iowa, and it provided me with a new address. Of course, a magazine will not do this without a valid reason. I had to use the name of the credit card company to get the magazine employee to shake loose of the address, knowing that the magazine would not like to lose the right to have subscribers charge their magazines to that credit card.

The garbage of a parent is also valuable. A toll charge on the phone to a son or daughter or a letter can resolve a skip.

ITEM #5 PERSONS LIVING AT SAME ADDRESS

If you were to have the advantage of this information at the beginning of your search, your job would be easier because of it. I would estimate that thirty percent of all the skips I have found in my career have been single persons who were living in their own apartments or sharing with someone. Many times, these roommates are co-workers, fellow college students, or just good friends. Any one of these can either take you right to your skip or provide information which will lead you in the right direction. As mentioned before, you may even have to skip trace the roommate to get the information you seek. He has a lot of information for you if you can talk to him. He may know where the subject is from, his brothers' or his sisters' names, where he was or is working, or his new address.

During the period of time that I lived in Kansas and owned a collection agency in Kansas City, I was making collections on student loans for a university. Many times I resorted to roommates for information. Rarely was I left without some lead or another. The roommate may have had a phone listed in his name and allowed your subject to place long-distance calls. If he has the toll sheets, he can give you the numbers. If he has thrown away the toll sheets, he can call the telephone company and have it forward a duplicate set to you for as many months as he requests. One thing that he surely will know is the name of your subject's girlfriend. Whether you are provided with this information or develop it yourself, you will find that it is a good source.

Here again, you will not be able to just start asking questions at random and expect to receive answers. You must be able to give the roommate a good reason to believe that it is necessary or important to talk to you — especially in the case of female subjects who have female roommates. They, like mothers, are careful about whom they talk to and what they say to a stranger who calls. Do not be afraid to use deceptive pitches. I have found no law that says it is a crime to lie, except when lying to the government or hurting or defaming someone. When you are lying to gain information and your lie cannot hurt your subject in any way, what, if anything, have you done wrong? Telling someone who you are and why you are really calling will never get you any real answers.

ITEM #6 MAIDEN NAME (See Item #2.)

ITEM #7 AGE (See Item #3.)

ITEM #8 RELATIONSHIP

Knowing in advance the relationship between roommates will give you an opportunity to develop your pitch before you speak to them. It can establish the value of the lead to you, and you can decide if you want to use it now or later as a desperation move.

As you are assimilating your leads, you might want to make a determination as to the value of each and the direction that it may take you. Of course, you want to resolve your case as quickly as you can, so it is important that you choose your direction carefully to avoid a lot of unnecessary moves. Your leads that are still good information are going to be the most effective ones to start with. In most cases, you will find your skips with just a few calls if you use the most valuable leads first. Do not try to use this manual in a step-by-step procedure. It is designed only to give you direction in gathering clues.

ITEM #9 NAME PHONE IS IN

This will be a real surprise to some debtor who is coming in to try to trick your credit grantor into an account. If he had intentions of deceiving, getting hit with this question will make him think twice. However, let's assume that this person was honest and intended to pay back the creditor at the time he wrote the application. He had no objection to filling out the application at the time because he had no deceit in mind. This information is just another clue for you to work with if the telephone was not in his name and he provided you with the name of the other person. Then again, he may have lied to you. It is your job to find out, and as we mentioned in Item #4, there are ways to determine this.

ITEM #10 ADDRESS

Whether or not this was truly the subject's address, this is where it all begins. I have indicated that you may find out the subject was hiding behind someone else to hide the truth about himself. In an effort to deceive his creditors, he may have used others, even good friends, to provide you with information which would make your job difficult. I should really say that he was making the collector's job difficult. The debtor does not know about us. I am glad that he does not because he has already been educated enough in ways to deceive creditors. Searching the address is a relatively easy matter. It is what you may learn that will take you on your way to the clues. Things that you will want to establish primarily about the address are the following:

Was this his mailing address?

Did he own or rent?

If he was living with someone, who was it?

If he was renting, who was the landlord?

If it was an apartment complex, was there a caretaker living on the premises?

Was a rental agency managing the property?

Where did he come from?

Where did he go to?

Who were his neighbors?

Who was his favorite neighbor?

These areas and others that you may think of are the clue-makers in your search of his address.

Did He Own or Rent?

If he was the owner of the house, you may find that he still is renting it out to someone else. A call to the current tenant could answer this question for you. You could also contact the area tax assessor, who can tell you the owner's name or the name of the previous owner. When you are making contact with the tenant, your first question, of course, is, "Where can I contact him?" You might have to give this person a reason for your inquiry if you are asked, so be ready with one. "I understand that this property may be going up for sale," or "I represent a buyer who may be interested in this property," are a couple that I have found to be satisfactory. Once you have won his confidence, you might ask him any number of questions. Be sure, however, that you ask the most important ones first because, as you bleed him for more information, he will become suspicious and offer you less and less. This may be an important item for you to remember whenever you are about to ask questions of anyone. Win his confidence, ask all of the questions you can get away with, and then try to disqualify your subject by making a statement that would indicate that the matter no longer is valuable information.

Many times I have disqualified a subject after getting all of the answers I could. First of all, I probably have agitated the person being questioned by my insistent inquiries and have made him wonder if my purpose was legitimate. If I were to just say "thank you" and hang up, that person may find it necessary to contact the skip and tell him about the conversation. You never want to alert your skip that you are on his tail. A long time ago, I was talking to a skip's mother and found that she was very agitited. She had given me all of the answers that I needed to resolve the matter. However, because I had been using a rather illicit pitch, I felt that I had better use a disqualifier to erase her suspicions. I told her at that point that something did not seem to be right and indicated that it was possible that I had not even made contact with the parent of the proper subject. I made up a date of birth that would have made the subject I was looking for much older than her son and asked her if her son was born on that same day. Of course, the answer was "No." So, I apologized for taking up her time and ended that conversation.

Using a disqualifier at the end of a *hot* pitch can keep you out of trouble. I was watching the evening news once, and the consumer reporter came on with an elderly lady who was talking about a phone call she had received concerning her daughter. She told the reporter about all of the personal questions the caller had asked and was suggesting that someone was after her little girl. This is the kind of publicity that we do not need in our trade, so I have always used a disqualifier since then.

Maybe the house, if owned by your skip, is now up for sale, even if no one is living there. It would be listed somewhere on the real estate market, and you could contact the real estate agent. Another way to find out who is selling the property is to have a neighbor look at the real estate sign if you cannot get there yourself. Several times, I have gotten numbers off of "home for sale" signs and found either the skip at the other end of the phone or one of his relatives who was taking the calls.

Real estate agents are often hard to deal with, as they are suspicious of your reason for calling. Because they fear that you may be another real estate agent or may try to make a deal with the seller for whenever the listing runs out, they are reluctant to give you the information about the skip. Sometimes they will cooperate with you without question. Usually, it is to your advantage to use a ruse. I personally like to go out with them to the property to see it on the pretext of being a buyer and ask my questions casually. Of course, there is always the chance that you may have to wait until the property is sold to get your information from the public record.

If the house looks like it has been recently remodeled, you might want to try to find out who did the work and contact them. They may have had to bill the owner at another address. If you are able to go the property personally, you might find that the skip had cable TV. A check with the local cable companies may get you a new address to which service has been moved. You might want to make an offer to these cable companies for skip tracing at a low rate just to have them for a source of information.

I assume that you have already checked the post office for a forwarding address during your general skip procedure. I would like to mention here that you must never, and I mean never, assume that an address given to you by the post office is truly a good one. Skips do all kinds of great things when they intend to hide. They have their mail forwarded to friends, who put it into new envelopes and on to them. They do the same with relatives. But remember, these are clues for you also and should never be overlooked. In the last fifteen years, mail drop addresses have become the nemesis of skip tracers. A smart skip can hide behind them for years and never be found. I told you earlier in this manual about the fellow with the magazine subscription. Mail drops are very slow to forward mail, and magazines are not forwarded unless postage is guaranteed. This guy had been hiding behind a mail drop address.

Many mail drop services also offer telephone service, and some of them will even tell callers that they have reached the subject's home, that he is rarely there, and that they will only take a message for the subject. I had one telephone service employee tell me that she was the man's wife and that she expected him home in several weeks. If I were an unscrupulous character, I think that her business would be a good one for me. I could call it "Tom's Skip Tracing and Deadbeat Hiding Service."

If He Was Living with Someone, Who Was It?

Again, we find ourselves starting our search with a second party whom we may even have to skip trace to talk to. As in the case of a roommate, this is a valuable source of information and should not be overlooked. Friends do not often rent houses to share, although it does happen. Girlfriends and relatives are generally the ones who share houses. Professional people, co-workers and whole families also commonly share houses.

If He Was Renting, Who Was the Landlord?

If your subject is a deliberate skip, he may have skipped out on his landlord, too. This may turn out to be a good source of information for you even though the landlord does not know where he went. The landlord may or may not have an application on the subject but usually does know something about the skip. He may know where he worked, who his friends or his relatives are, what kind of car he drove or whether he lived alone or with someone, or he may have saved some rubbish from the house or apartment. He may let you look inside the house for other clues if he has not yet cleaned it. He may agree to let you know who is still sending mail to the house or apartment and who is calling him for information besides yourself. He may even want to hire you to locate the skip for him, too.

A landlord with an application is even better. If he will allow you to have all of the information on the application, you may have all you need to solve your case. If he is reluctant to give you this information, tell him that you will let him know where the skip is when you find him or offer him a free prerental investigation on his next tenant. He may agree and also want to know more about your service. One thing that I like to firm up with him is that he will forward the skip's last or next phone bill to me so I can search it for toll calls.

The property may have been sold and have a new owner since your skip left. You may have to call the new owner or check the city tax records to get the previous owner's name.

Was There a Caretaker Living on the Premises?

A caretaker or apartment manager can usually give you the same information as the landlord unless he works for a large property management company and does not have access to the records. There are still many things that he can give you, however. He may know the names of persons that your skip lived with or the make, model, and license plate number of his car. The skip may have left something behind that will offer you a clue. He may even know the unpublished number of the phone that was installed in the apartment. If this phone number was transferred by the skip or his roommate to a new address or changed to a different number, you will know that your skip is still in town. Information will give you the new number. The caretaker may be able to tell you if there were any other persons in the building who associated regularly with your skip.

Was a Rental Agency Managing the Apartment?

If you find out that this is the case, you may suffer a more difficult time gaining any information about your subject. Property rental agencies are either very good record keepers or very bad record keepers. You generally will have to handle an agency as you would the landlord of the property. The agency is responsible to the landlord to install a good renter and usually is given the authority to try to collect the unpaid rent from a skip. This could be your door opener to get the agency to deal with you if it truly intends to pursue the matter. Many of them don't. Make the same offer you made to the landlord and you might find the agency cooperative. Again, you may find a new client that is interested in your services. The majority of clientele are built on just this kind of offering and upon recommendations of other clients. If you are really good at what you promise to do, you will find yourself receiving calls.

Where Did He Come From?

There are always those who skip for the first time. They are usually easier to find because they do not know how to hide their tracks. You will find that many of the skip trace cases you receive have a record of skipping out on their creditors and are pretty good at it. I could not tell you how many times I have been asked, "How in the hell did you find me?" My reply has always been, "That is my job." I didn't tell them how hard I had to work to get the clues I needed to locate them because I would never give them the pleasure of knowing that they were pretty good at it. Rather, I would like them to think that they made a mistake and always wonder what it was.

I spoke earlier about having to go backward in the history of a person to be able to understand him and continue forward. I guess what I really was saying was that the recent moments in a skip's life are not as important as those when he was less knowledgeable. If I can get into his past, I will gather much more information about him than he is offering now. A credit bureau report will give me that names of creditors up to seven years old or even older. Many times these creditors still have applications on file, and many times these creditors were not able to collect from the skip because they gave up trying to locate him. Companies are beginning to pop up around the country that have associated with the credit bureaus and are offering national searches of credit bureau files. The cost is reasonable, and they have the ability to search almost all of the country in just a few days. The best information you get from a credit bureau will be the oldest, but the recent information may be helpful, too. If your skip is not a regular, you may find the information that you are looking for quickly. What I usually try to look for is information that will take me back to the time at which he was still listing the names of his parents, brothers, and sisters on the credit applications.

Another easy way of going backward is to begin a search of all of the old city directories in the subject's last area or other areas that you have learned about. This may bring you the names of employers he has worked for. They also have applications and may still maintain them. The employer, an old one or a new one, may be able to tell you about any unions that your skip belongs to. I recall a case I had where I was looking for a missing heir. Not a big case, but because I have the attitude that every case is important, I found myself in a very deep search for this man. He had been a member of the postal workers' union and had been an inspector in the Chicago area. In any other matter, the postal service will not give out any information on employees, but with my silver tongue, I was able to arrange for my letter to be forwarded to the heir through the postal workers' retirement fund office. This man called me as soon as he received the letter, and I solved another case.

Where Did He Go?

Answering this question will not necessarily locate your skip, but it may put you on the right trail. Your first point of interest should be to determine whether he had any reason to stay in town. Of course, if he has a valid job, he surely would intend to stay in the area. Then again, you should try to determine if his employer transferred him to another area of the country. Salesmen, engineers, and chemists seem to be transferred more than others. Military personnel, once they have finished their basic training, have the freedom to move as they please if they stay in the reserves. Other transient employment areas are magazine, cookware, and encyclopedia salesmen; roofers; painters; and steel workers.

If you can establish the profession of a subject, you may be able to relate these items to him. For instance, in 1975, I was trying to locate a skip who was let go from him job only because he was part of a vast cutback. His profession was welding, and he apparently was very good at it. After searching the usual areas, I was struck with an idea that was even new to myself. I went to the area newspaper and procured copies of all of the want ad pages printed from the day of his dismissal. I called almost every welder ad listed until I got a hold of a personnel manager who was cooperative. Sure enough, the subject had in fact applied there but had been too late, and the job was given to someone else. Representing myself as the subject's old employer, who wanted to rehire the man, I gave the personnel manager I was talking to the reason to give me the information from the application. This to me was a new and exciting discovery. It was a reminder to me that we cannot ever stop trying to develop new ideas. As I mentioned earlier, a labor union is a good source of information, even if it is reluctant to talk about a member. A credit union is much better, as it also has an interest in the subject. If he has a loan with the credit union, he has probably tried to avoid it also. However, this is not always true; the subject often tries to keep a good relationship with his credit union, as he wishes to stay in his profession and relates this to his responsibility to the credit union.

Another reason an individual may try to stay in the area is because of a serious relationship. He may even be willing to change his profession for the right relationship and stay in the area. If I am dealing with a single person or a divorced one, I always try to establish the name of such a friend and the seriousness of the relationship. I may even find that the friend has also left a job. This generally would indicate to me that they both have left the area. The matter now becomes an aid and not a hindrance. Skip tracing a matter involving two persons gives me that many more clues to work with.

Who Were His Neighbors?

Out of convenience, we like to live as near to our parents as we can during those young years while we are still unsure of our direction in life. This is more often so with the ladies. I could not count the times that I have searched a block or neighborhood and found the parents of a skip living nearby, next door, OR IN THE SAME BUILDING! Many times, though, we are just trying to locate those individual neighbors who might know something that will be of value to us in our search. Questions I like to ask of those who have answers are the following:

When did he leave?

Who was his landlord?

Who was he living with?

What kind of car was he driving?

Did he move himself or was a moving company employed?

Had he rented a trailer to move?

Was there any particular person or family in the area to which he had close ties?

Any one of these questions that may bring answers will give a variety of clues to work with.

Who Was His Favorite Neighbor?

The previous question should have given you this answer. Virtually everyone will associate with someone in the neighborhood. Sometimes this question will lead you right to a parent or a relative and give you the source you need to locate the skip. Friends made in the neighborhood are often lied to by the subject as to why he is leaving and where he is going, if only to leave a good impression of himself. Even then, he often will leave some information that may be of value to you. It may be something he said about himself, his family, or his job. You should ask all of the questions that you can get away with before the neighbor gets agitated. Sometimes the friendly neighbor is asked to save the skip's mail for him or forward it to another address.

A reminder at this point is that you will have to deal with the person that you are questioning very carefully to get all of the answers you can before he becomes suspicious or angry. If you find that the neighbor was in fact close to your subject and that you are beginning to anger him with your many questions, you may want to use the disqualifying method I spoke of earlier.

ITEM #11 APARTMENT NUMBER

Although you may not see any value in this item right away, consider this: You've searched the city and cross-reference directories and are about to contact persons living in the same building. If you do not know what apartment your subject lived in, you may not get any answers — because he may have been known only as "the person in apartment 111." Have you ever observed an anthill and watched the ants go about their business? That is what an apartment complex reminds me of. However, there may be someone in the building who can relate to your subject by name. This is the person you are trying to locate. If you do not know the apartment number, how are you going to get anyone to go to the mailbox to see who is living in the subject's apartment now? It may be a previous roommate! Also, consider that the apartment may have been in someone else's name or an alias. If you do not know the apartment number when you talk to the landlord, he probably will not have any answers for you either.

ITEM #12 CITY

Generally this area poses little concern. The only problems that I have come across were when I had to search a directory or when I received a skip trace request from a finance company when the subject account originated in another city and was transferred. I worked very hard to resolve one such matter, until I found out that the subject had opened the loan in another city and had been moved by his employer to my area. The finance company should have been aware of this and should have supplied me with this information. I located the skip back in the city he was from.

Certain professions are required to be licensed if applied for within a city limit. Cab drivers, peddlers, bartenders, and others are required to have licenses if they want to work. Businesses are required to apply for occupational permits to have a place of business in the city. I have found both of these areas helpful. Quite often, a suburb is referred to as though it were the city and not by its true name. A city records search in Milwaukee, for instance, will not gain any information about a bartender who worked in West Allis, a suburb of Milwaukee. I would have to call the West Allis City Hall.

ITEM #13 ZIP CODE

I once was allowed to look at a house interior by a landlord who also wanted me to locate a skip for him. A skip who is moving out in the night or quickly will usually leave behind some rubbish. This particular skip was not really in such a hurry, and he left very little behind. The only thing I was able to find of any interest was an old telephone book with an address and a zip code written on the cover. I was able to track the zip code through zip code information at the post office and get the name of the city. Upon calling information for that city, I was able to determine that a person with the same last name lived at that address. Further investigation determined that this was the brother of the subject, and he was able to give me enough information to aid me in locating the skip.

As long as we are mentioning telephone books, let's look into a few things that I have discovered over the years. Where do *you* write down people's names and their phone numbers when you do not have a piece of paper handy? In the phone book. So do I. I, as you probably do, will write the information on whatever page I was looking at before I decided that I would have to call information. So, look at all of the pages. If you were to call me and give me the number of another person, I would probably write it on the front or the back of the phone book. Who this person is and the reason that your subject had to have the number is still what you have to find out.

Another time that you will find the zip code useful is when you want to do a postal search to see of the skip left a forwarding address. When you make this type of inquiry, do not forget to inquire also about any persons who lived with your subject. They may have found it valuable to make an address change. When making a credit bureau inquiry, you are required to know the zip code.

ITEM #14 COUNTY

Identifying the county in which I am searching, as in the case of the city, is important because I may have to search courthouse records or contact a county registrar for information. Counties maintain property tax records in some areas even though the city may do that collecting. Courthouse records and sheriff's department records are also maintained by the county clerk.

In certain areas of the country, such as in the state of Virginia, certain cities have maintained independent status and are not part of any county government. On a map, you would tend to see the independent city as part of a county. It is not; it controls all areas of government.

ITEM #15 LANDLORD

We have approached the landlord from several different directions so far, and each time we have established that he is a good source of information if we can get him to help. I have made it a career to try to find reasons to convince landlords of why they must help me. Not all landlords take rental applications from tenants or even keep records. Many of them are just grateful that the subject moved, and even though the subject owes rent, the landlord does not want to be reminded of him. This kind of landlord is naturally hard to deal with. I have been able to get a few of them to cooperate by promising to try to collect the lost rent money for them at no charge after finding the skip. Even then, they may not have any valuable information. It would be best to go on to better things.

Those who do have information and are willing to assist you in your search should be handled carefully, as they may be potential clients or you may have to contact them in future cases. If you find that a landlord is interested in locating the skip also and you promise to get back to him, DO SO! If you use his confidence and do not make the return, you will never be able to depend upon his cooperation again. One of my biggest clients is a property management company which has the authority to expend funds to collect unpaid rents from skips. I began my relationship with this company in just such a way.

ITEM #16 ADDRESS (LANDLORD'S)

If you have just a landlord's name and not his address, you may have to contact the tax assessor's office to find him, and those records may not be up-to-date. It is, therefore, very important that when you are getting information about a landlord, you also ask for the address.

ITEM #17 LANDLORD'S PHONE

The same applies here as with the address of the landlord. Although you're in possession of his name and perhaps his address also, you may find that he has a nonpublished phone number. When getting information about a landlord, also stress the phone number.

ITEM #18 HOW LONG AT THAT ADDRESS?

This item can suggest several things to you. It can tell you that he was doing pretty good for a long time, that his trouble came suddenly, and that he was unaware of it happening. Or, if his stay was short term and you find out that he has done this to a lot of landlords, you might then assume that he is often a skip.

I was involved last year with a rental company which had a sudden rash of furniture/appliance rentals and quick removals. A long and intense investigation in cooperation with the authorities disclosed that we were dealing with one culprit, who had many aliases and forms of identification. This fellow had the unique ability to convince cohorts into going to rental companies and contracting whole apartments of furnishings. These orders would usually include television sets, stereos, and video recorders. Once he had everything delivered, he would have a moving sale or take the merchandise to another location to sell. Although we were able to observe him in action while having one of the moving sales, we were not able to move in on him because he was not the one who had ordered the merchandise. For future reference, we took down the license plate numbers of all of the people who carried anything out of the house and kept him under observation. It was several weeks before he struck again. It is not uncommon for someone to order a house full of rented furniture, as there are many legitimate persons who travel in their business and stay in a given area for only a short period. We broke this case by comparing the many applications we had gotten from all of the rental companies involved, and when the cohort came into the store and placed the order, we were able to distinguish many similarities in the application to those we had. It was decided that we would fill the order and call in the authorities to observe the delivery point. They did just that, and within minutes after the delivery was made, the culprit arrived and went into the house. Two days later, the usual ad appeared in the paper. The police answered the ad and arrested the subject with all of the merchandise.

Many times you will find that the applicant has lied about how long he has lived at a certain address. He does not want to be turned down for credit because he may know that the attempts will appear on his credit bureau record as inquiries. He knows that this will alert other creditors that he has tried to get credit at other places and has been turned down for one reason or another. There are things that he begins to know are important to credit grantors, and he is willing to lie to make the application look good. (It has always amazed me how educated these people get.) Actually, the longer you are able to confirm that he has lived at that address, the better off you are. A long-term residency will offer you a better chance of finding people in the neighborhood who have gotten to know him better. Since this proves to be almost always true, your search of the neighbors should prove more fruitful.

ITEM #19 HOW LONG IN THIS CITY?

At about the same time as investigating the subject's term at the given address, it is important that you try to establish his term in the city. Again, he was trying to establish a feeling of credibility for his creditor, and he may have known that it would look better for him if he showed that he had been around for several years. If you find in your search that this was also a lie, you might want to check out the landlords he listed previous to his current one and see if they even exist. A simple check at the credit bureau or the Department of Motor Vehicles may tell you that he has recently come into the area. A person with this much knowledge will probably be wanted by creditors in other areas, and you may be able to pick up valuable information from them. You will also be spreading your reputation.

While I was watching the movie *E.T.* for the first time, I was reminded of the many skip traces I have done over the years. Home. It has so many times led me to a resolution. Somehow, they all do wind up in the home area, even if it is years later and they believe that all is forgotten and forgiven.

This reminds me of a client I had years ago, who is now retired — a lawyer who represented a large department store for collections of bad accounts. Over the years, he had accumulated hundreds of uncollected accounts, and he was able to gain judgment on many of them. Many notations on these files indicated that the debtor had skipped out of the area and could not be found. At first I approached these accounts with the idea that I would have to try to first establish the area to which they skipped. Calling the references that were still around from the applications, I soon found that some of the replies I was getting were that the subjects were back in this area and were living decent and good financial lives. They all but blew my mind. I started to look in the phone book for the subject skips and not only found many of them listed, but they were often living in the very good parts of town. I guess that these were the persons who felt that if they could get their creditors off of their backs for a while . . . . The very first one I contacted on the phone was the first to make a statement that was to become the most common: "I thought that was all forgotten about."

ITEM #20 IF MARRIED, HOW LONG?

The one weak spot in this application is that it doesn't ask for the names of former wives and if there were children from a former marriage. Any information is good information until you prove it valueless. Knowing where ex-wives and the children of a marriage are will often give you answers to your quest. Of course, this man, like many others, may still be paying child support and often pays directly to the ex-wife. More often, however, he is obligated to pay it through the county clerk's office in the area where the divorce took place. A search of those records may or may not get you information. If you have a source in that records area, you can get the current address of the ex-spouse.

It is also essential to know if a subject is currently married. While searching records, you might find that it is necessary to also give the name of the spouse for identification purposes. And, of course, knowing the spouse's name as well as her maiden name will offer you another source of information as mentioned previously.

The wife may also be employed, and as we mentioned, employers have applications. She may have her own credit bureau file listed in her maiden name that will give you the name of her past creditors, which have applications also. The term of the marriage may indicate that they may have children who are of school age and are registered in a local school. This is an area in which you will need an inside source if you expect to get any information. These records are held confidential for the safety of the children. If the family has moved to another area or out of state, the records are usually transferred to the new school district at their request.

ITEM #21 PREVIOUS ADDRESS

I would prefer this item to read "PREVIOUS ADDRESSES." It is a tedious job to go back into directories and records to locate older information about a subject. The more that you are provided up front, the easier your search will be. However, as we are the professionals, the last line of defense, we have to do whatever it takes to develop the leads we need. Some areas to obtain information on old addresses are credit bureau records, old phone books, old city directories, courthouse records, landlords, friends, and motor vehicle ownership records.

As we progress in this manual, we will approach each of these areas if we have not already done so. You may notice already that I have led you to many of the same sources of information in different items. I have done this because, while you are assimilating the original information you are provided with for each skip, you will have to decide which item is the most useful with which to begin your search. You may find that you have been provided a quick method in one item and less in another. Your efficiency will make you a better skip tracer and a faster one.

Before closing on this item, I would like to mention that each time you are searching out an old address, you must use the same method as you would on a most recent one. The subject may have left friends behind at old addresses just as he might have at recent ones. He may have lived near a parent or relative at the old address, too. If you find yourself having to dig this deep, again, leave no stone unturned.

CHAPTER TWO
EMPLOYMENT INFORMATION

ITEM #22 EMPLOYED BY

Whether or not you have the advantage of having this information, you will invariably have to develop some history of employment during your skip trace search. Knowing about one or even more employers first of all gives you an insight into the area of employment the subject prefers, if he has a profession, or if he is stumbling around in life looking for a place. Then again, you might find that he cares for little stability and lives only for each day to pass. It is amazing how many of these people there are. More than often, these are the kind of people we deal with as professional skip tracers. Amazingly enough, they are many times very talented individuals. Many of them have high intelligence, and almost all of them have a natural ability to unravel most problems. It is because of this ability that they take the chances they do in their credit lives. They need to have the same good things that other people have, and somehow they truly believe that they will be able to handle earning the money to pay for them. However, they have not learned the discipline it takes to be a steady earner, and they do not have the personal drive it takes to succeed. Then, there are those few who become intentful in their credit lives and turn to deceit and fraud to obtain the things they think they must have.

If you do find a subject's job or his last known employer, you will have to convince them that it is important that they give you the information off of his application. The information that you are looking for that the personnel manager might have is the following:

His last known address and phone number

In case of emergency, who was to be notified

His date of birth and Social Security number

His full name

The name of his spouse and children

His group insurance carrier

His union

His previous employers

His personal references

His skills

His hobbies and other activities

His military status

Correspondence in the file from inquiring employers

Qualification for unemployment compensation

Special friends at work

In your quest, you must get to know your subject as well as you can. In the event that your skip becomes a difficult one, the more you know about him, the more areas you will find to search in. All of the above questions are asked in an effort to provide an area in which to find further clues. You may never have to use many of them, but it is important that you develop the habit of asking for them, as the time will come that you will face that one case that is going to become more than just another skip. It will become a personal challenge — the one you must solve!

My first personal challenge was Eino S ____________. With only a name and an area he had worked in as a lumberjack in the 1930s, he was the first missing heir case I had, and I wanted very much to find him or his descendents. His name, I thought, was a very unusual one and I should be able to develop a file fairly quickly. How wrong I was. I worked on this case almost exclusively for almost six months, and along with not being able to develop a family profile on his name, I was unable to find out any personal information about him at all. No one nor any place seemed to have any information on Eino to give me — not even a small clue to start with. I began to feel that I was going to lose, and that bothered me. I couldn't lose my first missing heir case!

I knew I had to come up with something concrete, even if it was chancy. Yes, I was really desperate! I climbed into my car and drove to the area of Superior, Wisconsin. What I was hoping to find were records of logging activity during the years in which he would have been a young man. I expected to find hoards of information about multiples of logging companies. Instead, I learned by talking to the old-timers in the area that there had been only one company that did the majority of the logging during that time and that almost everyone in the area had been employed by that company in one way or another. I noticed one thing while talking to these old-timers. They spoke of old friends by name as well as you and I remember the names of pets we have had.

Although I found out that the company in question had long ago gone out of business, I began asking for the names of persons who had been in charge. I got my first lead after three days of asking questions. One of the old-timers told me that his cousin had been the person who was in charge of the crew assignments and also stated that if anyone knew Eino, his cousin would have.

He gave me directions to his cousin's house, which was located in Ladysmith, Wisconsin. In spite of the already late hour, I drove to Ladysmith and found the house, which was located in the country. It turned out that he, in fact, did know Eino and that Eino had not been a logger. He had been a carpenter, and it had been his job, along with others, to build the skids they used in the woods to pull the logs out or to the rivers. After listening to his stories for hours, and he had some really good ones, he recalled that someone had told him that Eino had been caught in a forest fire and had been badly burned. The same person had told him that Eino had gone to Duluth and was working at the Farmers' Co-op, although this information was years old.

Rather than going to Duluth, I returned to my office the next day and got on the phone. A lot of long-distance phone calls were made that day, and I talked to a lot of people. Eino had become sort of a town character and had apparently suffered some psychological damage from the forest fire experience. I was able to establish at least one positive address that he had lived at, but that whole area of town had been torn down and changed. I picked up another clue from an elderaly woman who had worked as a clerk at the co-op. Eino had been a penny pincher. He had put his earnings into savings accounts and lived a meager existence. She gave me the name of a banker who had called her one day to see if she knew where Eino had gone off to. She had not been able to supply him with any information.

I contacted the banker, who was still a banker. Yes, he remembered Eino. It seems that Eino had regressed further into the pschological problem he was having and had disappeared from the area, leaving behind a savings account at the man's bank. He had been trying to locate Eino concerning the disposition of the account because the money was about to escheat to the state. He never did find Eino, and the money did escheat into the state school fund. The money had never been claimed although several bounty hunters had tried to locate Eino.

I did find him. One of the things that the lady from the co-op had told me had stuck in my head. In spite of the handicap Eino was having, he was, at that time, one of the best horseshoe players in the area and played every day. I drove back to Duluth. Asking around at the horseshoe pits in the park she had named gave me all of the answers. I am not going to name the place in which I found Eino, other than that it was on a farm in the state of Minnesota. Although it was a small inheritance, I was able to get it to him. The funds that had escheated to the state were a different matter. Eino was not able to identify himself by other than the fact that his name was the same. His state of mind was such that any sworn affidavit he may have given would not have been accepted by the state as evidence of his identity. He no longer had any records to prove that the savings were his, and there had been no signature on file to compare with. I was told by the state attorney general's office that any testimony from the banker, even if he could identify Eino, would not be accepted. We made the claim, for the record, but it was turned down. My monetary reward for this matter was limited only to my actual expenses at my request. I had taken the challenge and won. This was my true reward. What I have tried to show you here is that there is a lead somewhere, and you have to find it. A clue brings another clue and so forth.

ITEM #23 JOB ADDRESS

It is not always certain that you will find the company you are seeking at the address provided. Do not despair if you look into the city directory and find that there is a completely different company named at that address. The thing that you may find is that the company named on your application is a part of the company listed or that the company listed is a cover for the subject if he said that he was self-employed. The company you have found may be an answering service or a mail drop.

Many companies have offices that are only for corporate business, although they may have plants or other offices in different areas. Generally, you will have to send your correspondence to that address to get any form of reply. A phone call, however, may save you a lot of time, especially if you can get a better location that your subject worked in.

Your credit grantor should have discovered any oddity at the conception of the loan and corrected it before he granted the account. However, as is often the case, it was assumed that the address was given correctly. This is one of the most usual areas that I have found in which to detect credit fraud attempts. Checking thoroughly on the job address can tell you if the subject was trying or succeeded in using a friend or relative for a job reference.

ITEM #24 JOB PHONE

The same rules apply here as in Item #23. The information should have been researched by the credit grantor. The telephone number could have belonged to anyone that he was able to get interested in lying for him, as was in the case of James B _______________.

I was working on a skip trace for a bank as a preliminary to a repossession. The subject had listed his employer as being a very large company which made auto body frames and stated that he had been a welder there for a long time. Everyone in that area was aware that this plant had existed for years and was one of the best paying in the area. The credit grantor made the mistake of assuming that the information was good, called the number given, and was given confirmation of all of the information that appeared on the application. I noticed that there was a disparity between the prefix of the phone number given and the prefix usually used for phones in that area of town. In checking further, I found that the telephone had never been listed to any plant or company in the area. I tracked the number through my collection of city directories and could not identify that it had been assigned to anyone during that period of time. It must have been an unpublished number, I determined, and after contacting my source at the telephone company, I found that the number had been assigned to the debtor himself, listed as "Children's Phone." Someone had apparently answered the phone using the company name and confirmed the job information. I have always had a suspicious nature, and I am reaffirmed to that belief over and over.

ITEM #25 OCCUPATION

The skill the subject says he has may not be the job he performs either. It is imperative that you establish the actual trade each subject has practiced. His ability to procure another job in this day and age may depend upon the previous experience he can show. Knowing this will aid you in your search as it did myself, as I mentioned in a previous chapter about the want ads. In another situation, finding that the personnel manager was uncooperative and knowing the area of work the subject was in, I was able to call the plant the next day and ask for the supervisor of the shipping department. There, I was able to locate friends and even talk to them.

ITEM #26, 27 and 28 All basically the same as ITEM #25

The more information that you are able to generate when questioning people, the better off you are going to be when it comes to trying to gain entry into the job area to get answers. Knowing how long the subject has worked on a job will give you some idea about how well he was known and also how skilled he may have been. Knowing the name of the department he worked in will give you even a better source of information than the personnel manager. Knowing the name of his supervisor will get you into the department without any hassle at all and avoids your having to answer a lot of questions while trying to get into the department.

ITEM #29 WORKING HOURS

Was it his preference to work these hours? Were these mandated hours? Either way, the hours he was or is working can give you some idea as to his off-hours activity. Those who work first shift have a lot of time for leisure activities because more are available during the off hours. For those who work on the second shift, leisure time is hard to find, as very little is happening during the off hours. Third-shift workers do have it a little better, as they have the late afternoon and the early evening available to them.

Your subject has developed habits that he likes to stick with even when changing jobs and will usually try to gain employment where he can work on the same shift. He is also reluctant to change shifts if he already has a job unless he is a second-shift worker. Considering his working hours and the activity he has available to him during his off hours may give you some insight into his lifestyle. If he is a first shifter, he likes to stop with the guys for a few. He will then go home, if he is single, and he will clean up and go do the things he has scheduled for his life — drinking with friends, sport activities, clubs, and other. Chasing a first shifter out in the field is difficult because his activity time is lengthy, and if you cannot determine any regular activities, you may be spinning your wheels.

One of the things I try to find out when asking questions at a company, whether the subject is still there or not, is if he was involved in any sport activity. Many times, if he was on a company team, he will be able to keep his position even if he no longer works there. Other members of the team usually become good friends and are worth your time to find and question. If you have done your job while asking questions in his neighborhood, you may have found out about some of these activities. Then you would have some positive questions to ask when you get into the job area.

Second and third shifters have less time, but they strive to have some kind of social life, even if it is a few last-minute drinks before the bars close or some early morning drinks at a superbar. Many third shifters like to stop at a restaurant for breakfast before they go home. Knowing the subject's shift hours also becomes important when you want to question co-workers going into and out of the work area.

ITEM #30 and 31

If you are a collector and are skip tracing your subject, I would suggest that you do not contact him until his paycheck is in his pocket. If you are going to be able to get him to pay up, this is the best time to do so, as he cannot deny that he has the money. Ask him too soon and you will get an excuse, or ask him too late and some other collector will already have his money. When you are dealing with a person you have just put so much time, effort, and money into locating, your timing should be pinpoint. Payroll department personnel may not be the most informed people in a company, but they do have information available to them that may help you. They know the subject's Social Security number. They know where his unemployment checks are sent to. They know where his final check was mailed to. They know who has garnisheed him. They know who voluntary wage assignments are going to. They also know the address that the subject gave them to send his earnings statements to.

ITEM #45 PREVIOUS EMPLOYER

Whether you gain this information from your contact with the last known employer or through some other source, such as neighbors, friends, relatives, or old directories, it is imperative when you are questioning any source that you try to gain this information. Once you have obtained access to the name of a previous employer, you will be looking for information that is quite often stored away. Be ready with a good reason with which to convince the previous employer that it is important that he find the old job application for you.

If you are successful in getting his help, the information that you are looking for is the same as the information that the most recent employer had for you. You want to learn his full name, his date of birth, the name of his spouse, the names of his children, the references he used, who to notify in case of emergency, etc. Do not forget to ask also for the names of the previous employers he listed on this party's application. You might have to go back even further.

You will also want to know if the previous employer has any knowledge of any good friends the subject may have had there or if the employer may have hired any of his family members. The further you find yourself going back into the employment area, the more difficulty you will have in getting these people to cooperate. That is why I remind you that you must have some very good reasons ready and well practiced. You cannot stumble!

Do not be surprised to find conflicting information as you go back into the past with these subjects. The more practiced they become in hiding from their creditors and filling out applications for employment, the more you will run into altered facts. The older the statements are, the more honest you will find they are. As they have learned what information is best to prompt credit grantors to give them credit, they have also learned what information is best for the personnel manager. They will only tell the good about themselves, and if they have none to tell, they will make it up.

Do they ever! Recently I was reviewing an application for a collector friend of mine because he could not get any direction from the information he saw. This was a copy of an employment application he had gained from the subject's most recent employer and it was only several months old. I could not believe my eyes! Everything on the application was, in some manner, a false statement. Even the college he listed was nonexistent. His address was a P.O. box, and the telephone number apparently had been a nonpublished number. I could not find any information that would have been immediately helpful. He had already done all of the preliminary work in his skip trace effort, including a motor vehicle and driver's license check on the subject. He had gained nothing. No clues!

It became evident that this subject had something to hide and had become very practiced at it. Because of the short term of the employment, I determined that the subject was probably on the run and was not from this area at all. For years, I have had the unique ability to smell out these kind of people from the information they give, and I advised by friend to use his law enforcement sources. He contacted me several days later and told me that he had found the subject in custody for violation of his federal parole. The subject had made a mistake. The name he used on the employment application was an alias he had used in the past, and the feds had arrested him as he was going into his job without the knowledge of the employer.

Other information that is available to you if you are able to locate old employers will commonly take you to other areas of the state or even the country. On almost every application I have reviewed where the subject had come from a farming family, the parent had been listed as a previous employer.

A missing heir case that I worked on several years ago might give an example of how hard we sometimes have to work to resolve our skip cases. I was contacted by an attorney who had been assigned a probate matter in a northern Wisconsin county. I was told that a gentleman who had passed away in that area had left a will indicating that his sole heir was his son. Unfortunately, he never was able to find his son and get to know him. He did not even know what his son's name was. The only information that was available was the name of the mother. The deceased had provided an address for the mother for the time that he had known her.

As it had been in the late 1930s, looking back in old city directories for this period of time was difficult because the city was changing its address system to compensate for the restructuring of the city blocks. I determined from old city records that the address I was given (933) was now located on the block that carried the 300 numbers. Looking into the directories from that period had only confused my search because I began contacting persons living in the current 900 block, which was five blocks north of the actual location of the house she had lived in. I had some vague memory of this change since I had grown up in the same area, but I had never run across the change in any of my cases. It took hours of searching through old city tax records and marriage records to finally come up with some answers. In 1939, the mother was listed at that address and her employment was given only as "seamstress." In 1940, she was no longer listed as living at that address and was not listed in the city directory at all. I checked the marriage records for those years and found nothing. A lot of hours later, having gained no clues, I decided to try to locate some of the old neighbors surrounding her at that time. This was not going to be an easy task because I would be looking for people who were by this time quite old. During my search of the records at city hall, I had made it a point to copy down the names of the owners of the other houses on the block, including the owner of the house she had lived in. In reviewing the information for the best direction to take, I decided that I would first check out the owner of the house she lived in, so I went to the Milwaukee County probate records room. As I entered the door to the room, the thought struck me that she might have also passed away. She indeed had. I pulled her probate file and searched for information which would give me a lead as to her son's whereabouts. She had left very little behind, and her probate had been a very simple one. The only mention of her son was that he had been listed as her sole heir, and the record gave no other valuable clues — except her address at the time of her death and the son's first name! She had died at a fairly young age, but her son would have been about twenty-eight years old at that time.

Upon returning to my office, I immediately contacted the DMV about driver's license records and found only one person listed in the state with the same name. The date of birth of this person was the positive factor as it was within the time that my subject would have been born. The DMV record indicated that the party was living in the city of Green Bay, Wisconsin. I checked the address from DMV through the Green Bay Public Library's ready-reference section and found that it was the address of a halfway house for alcoholics. I got the phone number and called, where I spoke to the director of the house. He informed me that my subject was a reformed alcoholic who had stayed at the home to help others and had eventually become the director himself. He had just retired and was about to move to the state of Arizona because of his health.

I was told that the subject was out of town seeing his doctor in Fond du Lac. I asked the director if he knew the name of the doctor and he gave it to me. THE DOCTOR WAS LOCATED IN THE SAME BUILDING AS THE ATTORNEY I WAS WORKING FOR. That was only part of it. I called the doctor's office and found out that the lawyer's office was just across the hall from it. The subject was seeing the doctor at that time, and I told the nurse to not let him leave until I called back and told her about his good fortune. She agreed and I called the attorney, who was as surprised as I was. The attorney personally went across the hall to the doctor's office and waited for the subject to finish his business with the doctor. When he returned to his office with the subject, he called me back on the telephone and told me that I had in fact found the right person.

My original intent in this matter had been to establish some employment history on the mother and track her through her jobs. As you can see, it was another series of clues that took me in a different direction to solve the case. Since it was just a few days before Christmas, I have always referred to the case as my CHRISTMAS STORY.

ITEM #46 HOW LONG WITH THE PREVIOUS EMPLOYER

Basically, what you are looking for is whether your subject is or has ever been stable in his employment. It is, as mentioned before, important if you can establish a reason why your skip is gone. If he is a beginner, you may have more valuable information on him than you think;

and your job, if you direct yourself correctly, can be much simpler. If he is a regular skipper, short-term employments are good indicators. Of course, long-term employment will indicate that there were probably several good friends there who may be able to help you. Your goal is to out-think the subject, and the more you can learn about him, the better you will be at asking questions about him.

ITEM #47 THE PREVIOUS JOB PHONE NUMBER

Handle this phone number just as you would a current one. One difference that you will have to consider will be how long ago this number was valid. If you were to call that number and someone answered using a different company name than you expected, would you say, "I'm sorry," and hang up? I hope not. Companies sell out, change names, and quite often keep the same phone numbers. Ask before you leave the line. When you are asking questions of a recent employer about a previous employer, always ask if they have the phone number, too.

In closing on the subject of employment, I would like to remind you that a great part of your success as a skip tracer relies on your ability to create new sources of information and maintain them. Certain employers which have a steady turnover of personnel can be valuable sources for you in the future. I mentioned earlier that I had been able to locate a skip by contacting a personnel manager who had run an ad (help wanted) and found that my subject had applied for the position. Having an "in" at major employers in your area may someday benefit you. Protect your source of information at all costs. Never let anyone know that you have the source.

CHAPTER THREE
OTHER INFORMATION

ITEM #48 WELFARE/OTHER INCOME

Since the availability of easy credit, even welfare recipients have been able to obtain open credit accounts. These are the people that most often relocate, and they may move on the average of two times each year. The reason for this may be that they, in spite of their inability to face the responsibility of working for a living, still want to have the nice things that others have. Clothiers, furniture stores, TV and appliance rental stores, and others have made it possible for these people to have these nice things. Even though their losses are high, these stores deal in such high-volume sales that the losses are absorbed by other customers, collection activity, repossessions, and low costs through volume buying.

It is this type of skip trace that brings us the least credibility as it is the hardest for our clients to collect or repossess from. As I mentioned earlier, welfare records are generally held as public information, although you may have to search your state's statutes to find out how you may get access to them. It would probably be wise on your part to try to establish several contacts within the welfare agencies in your area. Going through the "channels" is usually time consuming, and your contacts can probably get you the information much quicker.

There is a lot of fraud in the welfare system, and you will run across it often. Becoming aware of a fraudulent situation in this area may be your in with the fraud squad in your area. This is an "ice cream and cake" job for the law agency that controls it, and those individuals who are assigned this duty quickly become very lazy in their job and depend upon tattletale reports before they open an investigation. They are very appreciative of the information you give them, and you can develop a very cooperative source of information for your needs.

One case I recall very clearly was a skip assigned to me by an Indiana bank on a woman who apparently had a number of relatives in my area. The bank did not know if she had come this way but, on the chance, had hired me to check it out. Apparently, it had given her a loan for a new car and she went delinquent on the very first payment. She had been a nurse in the state of Indiana and had worked at a hospital for a number of years. Outwardly, it was a good loan and would have been granted by any credit manager.

The truth, however, was that this lady was part of a welfare fraud group working in several states. I found out this information much later. Because of the nature of the quick way she had skipped, I decided not to make the usual contacts with the relatives so as not to alert her. At this time I did not have any knowledge of the welfare situtation, so I had no reason to search in that direction. Because she had been a licensed nurse in the state of Indiana, I checked my state's licensing board to see if she had made application there. She had not. I checked out all of the private nursing services in the area to see if she was working for one of them and could not find her in this area either. I decided to take another look at the information I had been given by the client and decided that it had not given me enough information to use.

I contacted the bank and asked it to get me the informtion regarding the automobile. It responded by giving me the VIN, the license plate number, and the color of the car. As the bank had already checked Indiana's DMV and found no change in the registration, I knew that it would be useless to check Wisconsin's DMV. I only had one way to go — the license plate number. I contacted my source in the police department and had him run the license number through the computer for parking violations, especially overnight violations. He gave me several violations that were listed. All were overnight. All of them were on the same city block. I first checked the addresses of the relatives the bank had given to me to see if any of them lived anywhere in the area where the tickets had been issued. There was nothing even close. I then checked out the block through my street directories and found that there were three private homes and two large apartment buildings. I contacted the management of the apartments and was told that, to their knowledge, a person answering her description and driving a car such as hers had not moved in. I decided to drive to the area and do a block search.

The first thing that I noticed was that the apartment buildings had very little parking space available and that what was there probably was for the tenants only. I drove through the parking area anyway but found no sign of her car. I cruised the area in a rotating fashion for several blocks in every direction, knowing that I had found cars located as many as eight blocks from the residence in the past. I didn't locate her car.

I returned to the block where the tickets had been issued. Two of the tickets had been issued to the car while it had been parked in front of one of the private residences. I went to the other homes on either side of the suspect home, and although one of the residents seemed to remember the car, she informed me that all of the other private homes were occupied by elderly persons who had lived there for a number of years. She also stated that the people who lived in the apartments were always getting tickets on this street and that there was often not enough parking for the tenants because sometimes several car owners would live in the same apartment.

I left a card with her in the event that she saw the car. I continued an early morning and evening hour surveillance of the block, changing my hours each day. The tickets had been issued at different times of the night, so I could not depend on any particular time. I got my break on the fifth day. It was a Sunday and I was about to leave to do the block searches in a number of cases. The lady I had left my card with called me and told me that the car was parked on the street outside of her home. I drove over there immediately and put the car under surveillance. I parked in such a manner that I could see which of the three buildings anyone would come out of. Being a Sunday morning, there was not a lot of coming and going, and it was not until about 11 a.m. that I observed a black male come out of the apartments and go to a car in the parking lot. He removed something from the car and returned into the building. Several minutes later, he came out again with a black female and got into the same car and drove off. More and more activity started as it got later in the day, and I began to think that I would be there overnight. I kept on waving at the lady who had called me, as she was looking out of the window every so often. It was about dark when the black couple returned and went into the building. It was about twenty minutes later when the black woman who had been with the man came back out of the building and walked up the street to the subject car. She climbed in and drove off. I had no reason to follow her at this time. I drove through the lot and took down the license plate number of the black man's car.

The next day I ran the plate number through DMV and identified the man. He was listed as a tenant in the apartment building. When I called the manager of the building back, he informed me that the woman in question was, as far as he knew, the wife of the man and gave me a completely different name for her. I ran this name through all of my sources and discovered that she was a welfare recipient and had been on the welfare rolls for several years. I contacted my source on the fraud squad and told him of my suspicions. He checked her under the name she was using in several states and found that she was getting welfare in Michigan, Indiana, Illinois, and Wisconsin.

In locating my skip, I opened up a whole new can of worms. Several weeks later, my source contacted me and told me that because of the information I had provided, not only had they broken up a large welfare fraud ring, but the man she had been living with had been wanted by the feds and they had arrested him. This is the stuff that will gain you sources of information that will make your job much easier.

ITEM #49, 50, 51, 52 and 53

As in our search in employment information, this information, if you have it available to you or if you are able to develop it, will only help you get to the inner source of information in the welfare department, and you will still have to develop ways of abstracting information from that source.

When you have made contact with an inner source, such as a case worker, the more information you have about the subject, the more he will believe that you have a legitimate reason for calling. If you are vague about your subject and have very little information to give, the case worker will feel that you are simply fishing and will tell you little more. Be prepared. Never inform him that he has a fraud situation on his hands, as it was more than likely he who made the initial investigation into the eligibility of the client. Then again, he may have something more to hide!

The very first welfare fraud case I ran across was by accident, and I was so new in the business, I did not know how to handle it. I was searching for a young woman for a local department store. The skip trace was easy and I found her within minutes. However, the skip trace request included a request for a job or assets. Unable to come up with any information of this kind on her, I made a late night visit to her trash can and took the contents back to my office. I found a number of empty envelopes that I was able to identify as welfare check envelopes as I had seen them before. There were, as I recall, about seven of them and also advice slips for different women, all in different amounts.

Very curious, I contacted the welfare information phone the next day and confirmed that all of these women were receiving public help and all of them had the same case worker. My inquiry also must have raised some question in the mind of the girl I made the inquiry to, as I received a call from a fraud squad investigator only minutes later. He asked me where I had obtained the information and when I told him, he asked me if he could come over to my office and see me. I gave him all of the material I had found in the trash can, and he went over to the department store with me, where we searched the files for credit accounts for all of these women. There were four accounts — all in different names.

When the investigation was completed, it turned out that the case worker had developed almost two dozen welfare files in different names and used her three daughters to act as recipients. Each of the daughters received several checks each month in various names.

I have become involved in several cases over the years that have led to similar results. One was a man who was dropping off women at the welfare department to pick up food stamps for him, although in their names. He would then trade the food stamps for cash value less a percentage at a small grocery store, which had an owner who was willingly involved. Another situation was a A.F.D.C. (Aid to Dependent Children) case where the welfare recipient would borrow children whenever her case worker was coming over to visit — when, in fact, she had no children of her own. Remember, the fraud squad investigator you are working with is guided by a "take but don't give" policy, and you must never disclose this source.

ITEM #54 and 55 WHAT IS YOUR HOME TOWN? PERSON TO CONTACT THERE?

What great information this would be if we could be gifted with it each time we receive a skip request! However, if our clients had this information, we would not be needed. In every conversation we have and with every area we search, we should look for this information. I have always referred to this information as nucleus information because it takes us back to the beginning of an individual's adult life. Earlier in this manual, I mentioned the value of this information when your case is too fresh to skip forward and you will best benefit by going into the past. Without clues to lead you into his past, this is one area where you will have to be resourceful and imaginative. Some of the areas in which I have been able to develop clues are the following:

CONVERSATIONS WITH FRIENDS AND NEIGHBORS

CORRESPONDENCE FROM OTHER PERSONS WHICH HAS BEEN LEFT BEHIND IN TRASH OR OTHER PLACES

EMPLOYMENT APPLICATIONS

CREDIT APPLICATIONS

RENTAL APPLICATIONS

OLD DMV VEHICLE RECORDS

DRIVER'S LICENSE RECORDS

TELEPHONE TOLL SHEETS

ABANDONED CARS?

I threw in abandoned cars because it reminded me of a very quick skip trace I did not too long ago for a bank. Arriving at the house of a skip (after he had skipped) to ask questions of the neighbors, it was pointed out to me that the subject had abandoned an older car in the garage belonging to the house. I looked at the car and noticed that the dealer sticker was from La Porte, Indiana. After going through the neighbor interviews, I returned to my office and called the dealer in La Porte. He was extremely cooperative as he had carried the down payment money on his books and the man had skipped on him several years before. He gave me all of the information off of the application he had taken, which included the name, address, and phone number of the man's mother. I called the number. THE SKIP HIMSELF ANSWERED THE PHONE!

Once you have developed a good idea about where the skip is from or, sometimes, where he has been before, you have several directions to take: same last names, old city directories, old phone books, bars, clubs, banks, co-ops, credit unions, employers offering jobs in his trade, and DMV information in other states. You can just about rely on the fact that if he was involved in some job, activity, or other in the place he skipped from, he was also involved at the place he came from as well as the place he is headed for.

Understanding your subject as well as you are able to with the information you are able to obtain will give you the direction you need to be imaginative enough to think into his past as well as into his future plans. I like to create a mental profile of the subject out of the things I have learned about him and try to imagine myself as him.

A friend of mine once told me that he would never go back home to Pittsburgh unless he became successful. He became a consistent skipper from many areas of the country before he decided that home might give a fresh start with new ideas. How many times does a failure have to fail before he goes home? There is no answer to that question, but I know that he will go home sometime. The older he becomes, the less apt he is to return to the place he came from, usually because there is no family left. However, the younger skips have no reluctance to returning home because they have family there.

ITEM #56 THRU 61 SOCIAL SECURITY NUMBER, BIRTH DATE, DRIVER'S LICENSE NUMBER AND PHYSICAL DESCRIPTION

Social Security Number

528? 440? 237? We are a society of records. From birth to death, records are being compiled about us and stored in drawers and computers. We are given a number at the hospital when we are born, a number when we start school, and a number when we go to work. Can you imagine your surprise if I were to come up to you and call you "528"? I would in truth be calling you be the nickname of Utah. If I were to call you "440," I would be referring to you as Oklahoma. If I called you "449," you would be answering to the name of "TEX." Your Social Security number is issued to you with reference to the state you were in when you applied for it. In almost every case, this is the state that you were raised in and have left some family in. You would have also left other records that I should be able to discover simply by knowing your number. Because your Social Security number is one-of-a-kind number, it has become the most commonly used "identifier" through all areas of your life. There are those who believe that in the near future, all and everything you own or do will be controlled by your Social Security number.

I could tell you about a number of cases I have solved only because I was able to have or find the subject's Social Security number, but I think I will tell you about a department store client that gave me an unbelievable volume of skip trace business. The majority of it was basic skip tracing, and I was able to resolve many of the cases quickly. About a year went by and I found myself working on the dregs left over. I noted that twenty-seven of these had Social Security numbers from the state of Illinois and others were mostly from nearby states. I grouped them in piles by state and sent a general inquiry letter to the Department of Motor Vehicles for each state. I gave them all of the information I was able to for each of the individuals and explained to them the purpose of my inquiry. I sent along my check for the appropriate fee on each request and self-addressed, stamped envelopes for the replies. Within thirty days I received replies on all of the inquiries with some positive information on all but a few. The information provided to me enabled me to resolve almost all of the skips by researching the areas that they had come from.

Occasionally you are gifted with a Social Security Number from a client that may have been given to them wrong, was written down wrong, or is just fraudulent. I have always tried to get at least one confirmation of the Social Security number before using it as a lead. One quick indicator of a fraudulent Social Security number you might be aware of is if the number given does not correspond with the "home town" state.

Several states are adopting the Social Security number as the driver's license number. You may also be aware that the military uses Social Security numbers as I.D. numbers. There is a new development in the credit reporting business that is interesting, and although some have failed because of the lack of interest, there may be near you an agency that has the capability to search the complete national credit bureau files using the Social Security number. You might want to contact your credit bureau and see if it is leasing this program out to anyone.

Date of Birth

Also used as a common identifier, you should treat this item as in Item #3. One thing I would like to make you aware of here is the fact that there are juniors and seniors with the same name. There are also different persons with the same name, including the same middle initial or even the same middle name. If you are not aware of the actual date of birth on any individual, I would ask you to be cautious and not accept a same name as your subject until you are able to confirm his true identity.

Do not be surprised if you someday find two unrelated people with the same name living at the same address. It happened to me! When you are handling a missing heir case, you will find that without the true date of birth, you may never be able to properly identify your subject. You should always make it a practice to establish your subject's true date of birth before you start searching records. All probate records identify the deceased by date of birth and, in most cases, Social Security number.

Driver's License Number

Although every state maintains public records in this area, not all of them are openly willing to give out this information. But they must, so there is, at your request, a method within their rules to obtain it. If you are going to use this source of information, I would suggest that you contact them prior to your actual inquiry and find out the requirements and the cost. As in Wisconsin, some states will allow you to establish open accounts and allow you to get the information over the phone. You might inquire as to whether there is such a circumstance. You will probably be asked to explain why you want this information and will have to maintain a monthly account with a minimum fee.

From state to state, driver's licenses are issued for various periods of time. I believe that the general rule is four years. Some of the information that is compiled by this department is as follows: full name, including middle initial; date of birth; last address issued to; driver's license number; renewal date; and list of violations and where they occurred. Other information that most states require but is harder to get includes home phone number, occupation, place of employment, race, and physical description.

You may or may not be able to obtain a list of codes used which will identify the violations indicated on the report. It is important that you learn to read these reports since the kind of violation will indicate to you whether there was an arrest made at the time. Arrest records for traffic violations contain valuable information that may lead you to your skip. He may have been or even may be in jail. He may be going to traffic school. He may have been asked to give the investigating officer a local address. There may have been an accident involved and therefore a police report on file.

To show you how this information can work in your behalf, I will relate this story to you. I was skip tracing a subject for a repossessor and it became obvious that he had left the state. All indicators pointed to the state of Arizona. However, when I ran the subject's driver's license record, I found several recent traffic violations reported by the state of Michigan that had occurred in the city of Grand Rapids. One of the violations was OWI (Operating While Intoxicated). I contacted the Grand Rapids Police Department and told them about my case and that they had information that might help me. Although they do not like to give this information over the phone, I was able to convince them to, and they became very cooperative. The arrest record was read to me over the phone, and I found that the subject had given the officer an address in Jackson, Michigan. The automobile in question, which was the one I had been hired to locate, was still being held in the impound lot because the fines had not been paid. The auto was released to the repossessor when he showed evidence of the judgment for replevin and paid the fines.

Rewards come to you in many ways. Although you may say that there is a lot of luck involved, let me say that without your effort and imagination, this luck would never happen.

Driver's license records will also show you when a person's name has been changed, whether it is a legal change or a change from a maiden name to a married name. The maiden name is even harder to get if you only have the married name. Gaining a good source of information in this area is difficult, but you may have a source in the local police department who is able to get this information for you.

When you contact your state DMV, make sure that you ask and make a list of the information that they are willing to give you and what you must do to get it. Just having this knowledge will give your imagination a boost. Your information is only as valid as the dates that appear on the record. If the renewal date is just a short time away, you know that the information was given at the time the license was last renewed. When reviewing a driver's license record, you might want to make a note concerning the renewal date to remind you that at that time the information will have to be updated by the subject if he renews the license. If you have not located the skip by that time, you will have another chance, but give the DMV time to record the information after the renewal application is received. Another situation that you may encounter is that the driver's license record shows that the license has been surrendered to another state during application for license in that state. The record will show you what state this is but nothing else. You will have to contact that state for further information. Asking questions at every source of information will enlarge your idea vocabulary. Over the years I have developed a clue chart which I will relate to you later in this manual. You may try to make your own by using word relation.

Physical Description

I could not tell you how many times I have either found or eliminated a subject by using a good physical description. If I told you that I was looking for a man about six feet tall with brown eyes and curly hair, would you know that I was looking for a black man, about six feet tall with natural hair, a medium complexion and brown eyes? No, you would probably think that I was looking for a white man instead. It is important that you get as good a description of your subject as you can, and when you have to repeat that description, be as definitive as you can. When you are asking questions about someone and you are able to physically describe your subject, it quite often can prompt the memory of the person you are talking to.

Neighbors do not always identify persons by their names and, after receiving a good description of the subject, may be able to tell you something about him. Although one lady I was questioning did not know who I was talking about, when I pointed to the house that had the address that I had been given, she was able to respond when I gave her a description of the subject by informing me that I had the wrong house and pointing out the right house. I was able to locate the subject through information I received from the owner of the house. Had

I not been able to describe the subject with information that I had gotten from a co-worker, I may never have solved this skip.

As you progress in this profession, you will find that physicial descriptions will become even more important. There will come a time when you will be asked to locate a person that only is described to you. You will have to become proficient at asking questions that will get you the most accurate and usable description. I have found that using a sequential method has worked for me. I first ask, "Is there any particular thing you remember about the subject?" Then I ask questions about the following:

HAT OR CAP
COLOR OF HAIR
EYEBROWS
GLASSES
COLOR OF EYES
SIDEBURNS
NOSE
MUSTACHE
MOUTH
CHIN
BEARD
NECK
UPPER BODY
WEIGHT
BODY DESCRIPTION
LOWER BODY
LEGS
CLOTHING

ITEM #62, 63, 64 and 65 CHILDREN, AGES, GRADE AND SCHOOL

Whenever you are questioning a person about your subject, you are striving to obtain any information you can get, even though you may never use it. Information about a subject's children is usable if you are ever driven to the edge and have to use it. I would not advise using this information, however, until you absolutely have to. The public and the officials have become very conscious of the many child-snatching problems in the country. Your questions will arise suspicions in every area unless you have properly prepared your approach to the subject with the person you are speaking to. Asking questions of school officials and your sources for this information should be limited.

I would like to say here that you should never get involved in a child search that involves separated or divorced parents. No matter how you look at it, child snatching is a violation of a court ruling, and you will become involved in a matter that may cost you thousands to defend or may even put you in jail. If you are ever asked to find a child in relation to custody, go to or contact the court where the custody was decided and read the file yourself. It is not beyond a parent to show you a set of falsified papers which say that he has custody. It is very good-paying work, but be very sure!

If you are allowed to speak to the neighbor's children, those who were around the subject's children, you will gain the most valuable information. Children like to announce that they are moving and often tell their friends information that can give you a lead to where they have gone.

In 1969 I was living and working out of Kansas. I was contacted by a child's grandparent, who had been given custodial rights after the mother died in an auto accident. It seems that the father of the child had snatched the litte girl shortly after the divorce and the authorities had made little effort to find her. Because the child had been an infant at the time of the snatch and was now seven years old, the grandparent had virtually nothing to give me that would help. The only positive clue I had was that the husband had been previously married and had a son that had been about nine years old at the time of the snatch. All the client knew about the father was that he had been from Georgia and that her daughter had married him there. They had moved to Missouri, where the divorce and snatch took place. The client was able to provide me with a picture of the missing girl as an infant, and the picture included the mother, the father, and the father's son. On the back of the picture was written, "Mom, Dad, Charlie and Chad." The daughter's name was Charlie and the boy's name was Chad. The client told me that the daughter's name was really Charleen and Charlie was a nickname.

Having only this little information to work with, I decided that any other move than to use the information about the son would take me to a lot of dead ends. My first move was to go to the town where they had lived and ask questions of the neighbors. At first I could generate very little other than that some of the people remembered the family and had heard of the child snatch. My break came when I contacted the woman who had lived upstairs from the family. She had moved several blocks away, but one of the other neighbors gave me the location. Her son had been friends with the father's boy, and she suggested that I speak to him. I waited until he came home. I showed him the picture that the client had given me and he remembered Chad instantly. He told me that after Chad and his father had moved away from the mother, he would see them sitting in their car down the block occasionally. I asked him if he had ever spoken to them and he said that he had. Chad had told him that he was going to school in a smaller town several miles south of the city and that he really liked it there. He had also told the boy that he was making lots of new friends and was playing on a Little League baseball team.

I contacted the Little League registration office in St. Louis the next day and asked for a membership list. They could not provide me with a list of the individual members but did agree to send me a list of the teams that were registered for the current year and for the year the child snatch took place. When I received the list, I looked for any team that was located in a town just south of the subject's city. Within fifty miles, there were only two registered teams. Both of them were still active on the current list, so I contacted the coach of the one that was closest to the subject city. Yes, he did remember Chad and his father who had been active in the town's Little League and other activities. He told me that the father was a good man and was reluctant to give me any further information in spite of the reason for my quest. I suspected that he knew something, however, and I advised him that it would be better to deal with me than the police. He agreed and told me that although Chad had grown too old to remain in the league, he had become a fine athlete and was still active in sports at the local high school. I asked him about Chad's little sister, and he acknowledged that he knew of a sister but could tell me nothing of her.

Through the innocence and honesty of a child's memory, I solved a case that had been stagnant in the police files for years. I do not believe that they made any effort to find the snatched child.

A footnote to this story: after I gave the information to the grandparent and described the life of the little girl, she was wise enough to handle the matter on her own and not bring in the authorities. She made contact with the father and arranged only for visitation, to which he agreed. It turned out that the mother had carried an insurance policy for accidental death, and the little girl would be very wealthy upon reaching her twenty-first birthday.

ITEM #66 HOME OWNER'S AND RENTER'S INSURANCE

Mortgage companies do not like to give out any information about their customers. Trash cans have given me more. Home owner's and renter's insurance is transferable to other property. Insurance companies do not like to give out any information either. You may be able to get information from these areas on occasion, but you will have to develop sources in all areas of insurance. Insurance companies need skip tracers, and they are fairly easy to develop as clients. Agents are often easier to get help from. They also often know where the insured has moved to if the coverage was transferred, and they, too, can become clients for other matters.

ITEM #67, 68 and 69

This is another trash can item. I have found many banking records buried under the potato peels. Information you may find, such as out-of-town banks, finance companies, etc., can help you to develop leads. Getting information from banks is as hard as from mortgage companies, and you will do yourself proud to make as many clients as you can in this area. One of the best ways that I have found to get into banks is to keep watch in the *Daily Reporter* (the local paper where attorneys have legal publications) and watch for cases that involve banks. Many times I am able to call the collection manager at the bank and give him new information about his debtor. He appreciates this information because he likes to look good with his boss. In a case such as this, you also may have set yourself up with a new client, as he was not able to locate the skip himself. The next time you call him back for help, he surely will remember you. Auto loan collection people are the easiest to deal with in banks. They know the hard work that goes into skip tracing and feel good about talking to us. You might have to listen to a story or two, but if you let them talk, they will eventually get to the information that you are asking for.

A message to any bank collection people who are reading this manual: I do not consider you less of a professional than I or any other skip tracer in the country. You work hard for every skip you find just as we do. However, as your time is divided up into various duties, you are unable to give skip tracing the concentrated effort that we do. Because of this, you often have to go outside of your bank for help. Let me tell you that there are not too many of us, but we are spread around the country in such a manner that no matter where your skip has gone, you will find our kind of help when you need it. A recommendation: *Lawyers and Creditors Service Directory*, a desk-top, 1100-page forwarder's directory will give you contact with any professional you may need, including repossessors for every town, village, or city in the United States. *Lawyers and Creditors Service Directory* is also published by Professional Education Systems, Inc., and you can get more information about it simply by calling 1-800-826-7155.

ITEM #70 UTILITIES

Information availability from utilities varies in almost every area. In my area, it is almost impossible to obtain. At one time I was able to pick computer printout carbons from the trash bins of the utilities, but somewhere along the line they either went to carbonless forms or caught on and stopped throwing them away. I have been able to establish sources within the utilities and can gain most of the information I need. This information does change very rapidly and often. When a skip occurs, just as with the subject's phone service, he will use an alias to gain new service. I do not put utility searches in any area of value, although I do occasionally look there. In most cases, I am only using this information for confirming new addresses at which I have found skips.

ITEM #71 and 72 YEAR AND MODEL OF CAR — COLOR OF CAR

Gaining knowledge about your subject's vehicle is the start of a whole new direction in your skip trace effort. The color of his car may not seem important to you at first, but there will be times that you wish you knew it.

"The last time I saw my daughter, she was picked up in front of the house by an old blue car." That is what a distraught mother once told me when her seventeen-year-old daughter had been away from home for two nights. A few questions to her friends and the counselor at her school about the old blue car told me that she had been with a young man known to them as a drop out from the school who had picked her up after school in a car answering the description. The information was relayed to the police and the daughter was found.

A picture I took of a custom van, which I thought to be close to a witness's description, solved a case of boat theft for an insurance company when I showed the picture to the witness. The description of a blue van, with rust and dents and a yellow ramp, helped identify members of a motorcycle theft ring. Color has come into play for me many times in my career and will for you also if you have gained the information. Once, when I was questioning a neighbor, she insisted that she did not know anything that could help me. Then, when I described the subject's car to her and the color, she said, "Oh, that car! It moved around the corner."

A skip may try not to leave any traces of his disappearance, but there are always things that he takes with him. One of them is his car. The car, like his credit record, is like his signature and will always settle down somewhere. You must first discover what kind of car your subject is driving to start your search. As this area includes Items 73 and 74, I will go right on to them.

ITEM #73 and 74 LICENSE PLATE NUMBER AND STATE OF REGISTRY

This area will also include the VIN (identification) number. If you have not already discovered this information in your search or were not provided it by your client, you will have to utilize your right to the records contained in the Department of Motor Vehicles or the Department of Transportation, as it may be known in your state.

There are four areas in this department that will be of interest to you: alphabetical files; numerical files; title files; safety and responsibility (should have been covered in driver's license). Each of them will give you information that will be helpful to your search or may even locate your skip for you.

When contacting the alphabetical file, have as much information as you can ready for the research clerk. The clerk is able to search the entire file with only the subject name, but if you have no address to match with the name, you may not ever be sure that out of all the same names one of them was your subject. The clerk certainly will not give you all of the names and addresses unless there are only a few, and if he did, your search would be expensive and maybe fruitless. Generally, this department will maintain its records on vehicle ownerships for several years before they are deleted, even though the subject no longer owns the vehicle listed. You should be able to gain information about all of the vehicles owned by your subject that are on record. Each of these records will provide you with clues: other addresses he has lived at; co-owners (gives you contact to people who know him); lien holders (banks, finance companies, credit unions, etc.); and license and VIN numbers (takes you to another department for more information). When you are gathering information from this area, you will, as mentioned, have to try to establish some connection for the vehicle to your subject. If you have prepared yourself for this call, you will have in front of you the subject's last known address and all of the addresses that you are aware of. If you have a description of a certain vehicle that you know he has been driving, you could have the clerk scan all of the same names to see if any of them own such a car. If you are unable to establish any positive information on the subject and he has an uncommon last name, you might ask her where else in the state the name appears and where most commonly. If he is from your state, you might be able to get the names and addresses of relatives in this way.

I used this idea several times, and one case in particular that I recall was especially rewarding. I had received a request from an attorney in California to locate a man who had been a stock broker there, and the only information he was able to provide me with was that the man had mentioned to a co-worker that he had lived in Wisconsin. He had a very unusual last name, and as I was checking the alphabetical record, I found nothing on him but was advised by the girl that there were only three such names in the state, all in the same area. I got all three of them from her and, upon calling these, was able to establish that they were all related to him. I was told by one of them that the subject was in North Dakota. I found his phone and his address by calling information.

The information you will receive from the alphabetical file will take you to the other departments for additional information. A co-owner will take you to driver's license records (after you have checked out the co-owner's name for other vehicles owned). The license number will take you to the license file that may tell you about plate suspensions or about a plate transfer to another vehicle not yet registered in the alphabetical file. A VIN number will take you to the numerical records, where you will find the names of lienholders or discover the new owner of the vehicle. The new owner may be able to tell you something about your subject. The VIN number can also lead you to the title number, with which you can research through the title section and go back on the history of the vehicle all the way to the dealer.

Several times, while reviewing the title number and searching backward, I have found that the vehicle was purchased from another family member, which, of course, gave me the clue I needed to find the skip. Other times, I have found that the dealer that sold the subject the car also financed the down payment and had an application on file. Another time, I found the subject working for the dealer as a mechanic.

As in every area in which you are asking questions, at every source, take time to find out what is available to you and what you have to do to get it. Let me tell you about one that I have not yet solved and I don't know if I ever will. I like to refer to the matter as "Slick Skip." About a year and a half ago, I was employed to locate a skip that had purchased a new pickup truck and financed it through a bank. The bank was my client. For several months this subject had worked tediously at setting up a credit history in a phony name. By getting simple credit accounts, oil companies, department stores, MasterCharge and VISA, he was able to build a very credible file of creditors. Therefore, it was not hard to finance a new truck, especially since he had a high-paying job (also a phony set up) and a reasonably large deposit. The deposit check was drawn on the bank he was requesting the loan from. He was granted the loan and was allowed to drive the new truck off of the lot that same day. Then, he went to the bank and withdrew the balance of his account, moved out of his apartment, charged thousands of dollars on his credit cards, drove to Springfield, Illinois, and had his vehicle registered to a phony address, and picked up a new title by paying a counter-fee using the registration papers to authenticate the ownership of the truck. (How he got away with this, we still don't know.) THEN, HE DISAPPEARED!

There are many of these professional credit thieves out there, but this guy knew more than just the basic moves. From what I see, this guy had some experience in the credit/collection field. I would suggest that he got his experience in the banking field, probably in car loan collections. I only have one clue that may tell me who this person really is, and that is the auto he traded in to the dealer. I have someone tracking the information to see if it was registered to his real name. I hope that this is the mistake that he made. More than likely, if I do find out his real name, I will find plenty of records on him from the time when he wasn't so educated.

Just a brief mention here about the safety and responsibility section of your DMV. I believe that each state has such a department. When a driver is involved in an accident, is found to be at fault, and has no liability insurance, the state imposes a situation on him where he must post a bond to keep his driver's license. The bond is kept in effect for a period of one year to give the injured party time to make a claim. If no claim is made within that period, the bond is released. Correspondence between the state and the subject is available for your inspection, or you can get the address at which the department is writing to him. Two prime times exist during this period of time. They are immediately after the bond is imposed and just after the bond expires. When you find out that a safety responsibility has been imposed, contact the department and see if it has any correspondence going with your subject. You will also ask for the termination date of same.

License plates have to be renewed. When you are checking for a license plate number, make sure that you find out when the plate has to be renewed. Although many persons renew their plates at the counters of the DMV locations, the majority respond by mail to the renewal notice they receive from the department, thereby giving a new address for the new plates or stickers to be sent to.

Reviewing Items 71 through 74, if you ask the right questions and know what they are willing to give you, you should, in most cases, get the answers you need to resolve your situation. The following are the questions I would try to cover in each department:

ALPHABETICAL FILE:

Automobiles and other vehicles registered to subject

Addresses to which vehicles are registered

Co-owners on any of the vehicles

Same names in his area

Same names in state

Other vehicles registered to co-owners and addresses

Identification (VIN) number

License plate number

Subject's proper spelling of name and middle initial

(Do not forget that most states maintain this information for several years, and it is also available to you if you request it.)

NUMERICAL FILES (Identification or VIN #)

Ownership of vehicle

Co-owner

Addresses

Title number

Lien holder and location of

License plate number

Description of vehicle

Condition of vehicle (current license, title only, junked)

Is vehicle owned by a leasing company?

LICENSE FILES (Plates)

Plates registered

to ____________________

Address

Co-owner or leasing company

Identification or VIN number

Title number

Status of plates (issue and expiration dates)

TITLE FILES

Current owner

Address

Previous owner and address

Dealer and address

Status of vehicle

In this area, you may not have to ever use the information that you receive, but it's important that you obtain it. In the event that you have to dig deeper for your skip, you will not have to make the expenditure again to go further. Make notes! Do not think that your memory will keep all of the information that you have. I keep a skip trace chart of several pages on each subject, leaving myself plenty of room to write my discoveries for each category. This way I can review the file effectively for information I have found, follow-ups, and clues still open for research. All correspondence sent and all correspondence received is attached to the back page of this file so that when I review the file, I can confirm that all inquiries were properly answered. If not, I can follow up. Also, while reviewing the file, I will better be able to see the areas in which I have to call back and the dates when I have to re-inquire at sources.

CHAPTER FOUR
PERSONAL REFERENCES

ITEM #75, 76, 77, and 78 PERSONAL REFERENCES, ADDRESS, RELATIONSHIP, PHONE.

Mentioned many times over in this manual is your quest for information about the friends, relatives, and neighbors of your subject. You will find that in time your instinct will give you insight into where these people are. Places where you are more likely to find these people are the following: directories (old and new); phone books (old and new); applications; co-workers; other neighbors; other friends; same last names; same first names and initials; same areas; and same towns. You have to LOOK!

I have a collection of telephone directories that are regularly updated for every town and city in the state of Wisconsin and for almost every major city in the United States. I could not be effective without them. My sources of information, phone books, directories, and imagination are the tools of my trade. Just as a carpenter cannot work without his hammer and saw, I too need tools. Basic skip tracing, where a good, sound application or other information is provided, is not what I am talking about. The skips we get that are beyond the basic effort and the ones who are hiding — that is where we need our tools.

The most unusual way I ever found the maiden name of a skip was only two years ago. Amongst the rubbish left behind by a skip in a rental lease was a picture. It was a picture of a young girl and a man dressed in army fatigues. The landlord said that the girl looked like the woman who had skipped out. I was not able to develop any information on her from what the landlord had given me. I took the picture to a photo lab and had it blown up until I could read the name of the soldier on his shirt. It was only a last name, but it was a lead. I called the several same last names that appeared in the local phone book, asking for the skip by using her first name and the last name of the soldier. It worked. One of the answers I received was that the person I was talking to had a sister with the same name. I asked her if her sister also had the name used in the lease, and she replied that she had been married to a man with that name but had been divorced for several years. She was able to give me the phone number of the subject's best friend, who, when I called, gave me the new address of the skip.

Whenever I am looking into rubbish or at stuff left behind by a skip, I always look for the telephone book that they had used. I don't think that there are many of us who do not use the cover of the phone book to write down numbers of people we know.

I was looking through such a phone book once and found that several numbers had been underlined in the yellow pages under the heading of "City Government." Noting that one of the numbers was for the personnel department, I called the number and found that the skip was employed by the city as a secretary. Another time, an underlined number lead me to an auto service garage where a skip had a part-time job. Others were friends and relatives who gave me leads that enabled me to find the skips.

It is the number of leads, the imagination you have, and the way you follow up on those clues that will make you better at your job. Many times you will be able to locate relatives, friends, and such that honestly don't know where the skip has gone. There are other things that you may be able to discover from them if you will ask about the following:

Other Friends and Relatives

Bars

Clubs

Habits

Vehicle Descriptions

Wife's and Children's Names

Skills and Jobs

Hospital Names

Doctors' Names

Personal Oddities

I once found a skip after finding out that the subject's wife had been injured in a car accident and had to be in a wheelchair. The individual I was questioning knew that it was a rented electric wheelchair. I found the rental company which gave me the name of the insurance company, and through the information supplied by them, I was able to locate a record of a personal injury suit in another county. My client, an attorney, contacted the subject's attorney, and the skip was found.

Here again, in this category, you must ask all of the important questions. Make sure that you get all of the information that you can about your subject, including all you can get when the person is telling you about another friend, relative, or neighbor. Even the vaguest clue can sometimes be developed into new information.

"He had tons of credit cards! "This was a statement made to me once by a neighbor. I had already done my credit inquiries on the subject and had found very little. Amongst my list of clients are the local general credit card companies, so I called them and had them run the address of the subject through their delinquent account and skip files. I was rewarded with the name of a man who had given the same address as the one my skip had gone from, and the time span was the same. Comparing the applications received from the credit card companies and the one I received from my client, I found several identical items — enough to tell me that the person I had been looking for was using an alias. Armed with the true name of the subject, I was able to find him within a few hours.

It is not unusual for an individual to live close to at least one relative. If not the parent, a brother or a sister. This is more often true with a younger person, especially a daughter. Many times, when you are asking questions of neighbors, you will find that there is a relative of the subject living nearby. Although they cannot often give you the address of that relative, they sometimes can give you directions and a description of the relative's house.

When you are out in a neighborhood asking questions, do not pass up the playgrounds and the nearby parks. Kids know more about other kids than parents do. I once was lead by a teenager to the new house of a skip that had moved only to the other side of the city block. Another time, I was given the name of the paperboy who had told the youngster I was speaking to that the skip's son was still helping him with his route. Once I was told by a small candy store owner that a skip's son had mentioned that his family was moving to Chicago. This information along with a co-worker's statement lead me to a company in Chicago where the skip was working. I learned that he had been transferred to another area by his company, but the employer was uncooperative and would not tell me where. After learning this information, I called the receptionist at the local company office and asked her if there was an office in Chicago. She gave me the name of the company, an address, and a phone number.

CHAPTER FIVE
SOURCES OF INFORMATION

DEVELOPING SOURCES

Even though I have mentioned this item over and over, I could never say enough about it. Your success as a skip tracer may very well depend upon the confidential sources of information that you are able to develop along with the general sources that are available. I personally have enjoyed becoming involved in other people's skip cases. Helping them is helping myself. Often I have been asked to help locate a skip that I too had an open, unresolved file on, and the additional information helped me to resolve my case along with the other. Even if I have no immediate use for the information, I have found that I sooner or later receive a case on the same individual, so I store the information.

Communicating this closely with credit collection people and investigators has created an extensive BOOK OF SOURCES. This type of communication was instrumental in creating a valuable source of information for me at a very large factory. I once was contacted by the personnel manager. He called me on the advice of an attorney to help him locate a former corporate officer of the company. I was able to locate the man in just a few minutes and respond to the personnel manager. Since that time and never having to do another favor for him, the personnel manager has become a source of information for me on over 5,000 company employees and previous employee records.

Every prospective source may have one or more individuals with access to records that you need. The size of the company and the number of employees will help you to decide how many chances you may have to develop a source within its ranks. Picking the most valuable source first is important. A lesser source may not have access to all of the records that you may need. Go to the TOP OF THE LADDER first if you can.

How would you go about developing a source in a case such as this? I needed a source in a labor union (very hard to develop). I had to have a story that was convincing and would create a feeling of trust. I had to be able to give whomever I was communicating with a reason to feel that it was important enough for him to give the information to me in spite of the rules. The conversation went something like this: "Hi, Bill. My name is Tom Stelter, and I locate missing heirs and beneficiaries. I am looking for a fellow by the name of Norm Auschleger (a completely made-up name), and I was told by a cousin that he may have been a member of your union. I wasn't able to confirm this anywhere, but can you check and see if he was a member?"

He agreed to, and when he returned to the phone several minutes later and told me that there was no record of the man, I said, "You know Bill, my notes seem to be confusing. It says here that Norm was living with his uncle (give subject's real name). I wonder if the cousin meant that his uncle was a member. I'll bet you have something on the uncle. Can you check?" He did check and he found the record of the man I was looking for. He had committed himself to helping me and gave me the information.

I made it a point to call Bill back in several days and tell him that I was able to find the heir from the information he had given me and thanked him. I have had occasion to use this source again but have done so sparingly, saving him for only the necessary cases.

A liar? Yes I am! A professional scam man! My lies harm no one. They are designed to get answers where the truth will only bring rejection. I will never say that someone is sick or in an accident or any other potentially harmful statement to get answers.

In 1981, I was told a story that all but made me sick. Apparently a collection agency collector called a sister of a skip and told her that her nephew (her sister's son) had been involved in a terrible accident. He told her that he wanted to notify the parents (the skips). What the collector was not aware of was that the nephew had been all but raised by the aunt. Upon being told of the accident, she suffered a heart attack while on the phone with the collector. Realizing that something had happened, the collector told his employer, who called the police. Although she survived, she could have died.

This is the kind of distasteful tactic that cannot be tolerated in our business. Proper training and constant reminders to our employees can help prevent this kind of situation. The various regulatories governing our activities have a set of rules laid down for us. I do not always agree with many of these rules, but this one is a "no-no." Without scams, we are not able to do our jobs effectively. Using innocent, noninjurious scams will not bring attention to us, and as I said before, you must always have an escape ready if your scam is creating suspicion. Scams are built upon previous truths. Review the times that you have been able to locate someone using a truthful text and try to fit these situations and reasons into your current skip situations. You can alter your facts to make them fit. Just make sure that your facts are accurate and do not create suspicion in your listener.

You may have just done a credit bureau check on your subject. A wealth of information sources can be developed from what you have received. You note on the record that several creditors have rated him delinquent. You also see that there are collection agency activities and judgments filed against him. He is probably a skip with them also. The creditor wants to talk to him about his account. The collection agency wants to collect. The lawyer wants to execute the judgment. If you are in a deep search for your subject and all of the moves have not gotten you any clues, you will probably find yourself calling these people. Take advantage of these calls and try to establish a working relationship that will carry you beyond just this one matter.

"Hi, Charlie. I am skip tracing ______________________ and see by the credit bureau check that you may be looking too. Do you have any ideas?" At this point, if he has already found the subject and is collecting from him, he may be reluctant to give you any information unless you have already established a working relationship with him. He will not want you to allow other creditors to interfere with his ability to collect from this subject, and he may have even promised the subject that he would not reveal his whereabouts in exchange for payment on the collection account.

If he has not found the subject, of course, he will be interested in working with you and will probably give you information that has been available to him from his client. If you establish a working relationship and promise that you are going to get back with him when you find the skip, DO IT! If he ever finds out that you have passed him over, he will never deal with you again. You have established a permanent source of information. You have gotten information that was otherwise confidential. You may have established a new client for yourself. You can bet that he is going to put you on his calendar. If you have promised him a recall on any specific date, make sure that you do so even if you have not found the skip. You might find that he was able to develop other information or maybe even located the skip himself.

Have you seen this type of ad?

INFORMATION WANTED AS TO
THE WHEREABOUTS OF

____

REWARD OFFERED. CALL

____

Or, have you seen the ads lawyers put in local papers for judgment by publication?

STATE OF WISCONSIN
CIRCUIT COURT
MILWAUKEE COUNTY

SUMMONS

J.J. FINANCE CO.
-VS-
ZILCH AND ZILCH

To each person named above as a defendent. You are hereby notified that the Plaintiff named above has filed a lawsuit or other legal action against you. The complaint, which is also served upon you, states the nature and the basis of the legal action. [Etc.]

LAW FIRM OF BIG AND LITTLE

Both of these ads can develop new sources of information and new clients. The first type of ad, usually placed by the creditor, gives you a direct line inside those creditors' companies and to those responsible for the recovery of their delinquent accounts. If you have information that will be of help to those creditors, or if you can help find the debtors, you will have created future sources. Attorneys also place this type of ad when they are trying to locate missing heirs. Contacting an attorney may possibly get you involved in his case.

One of these ads that I responded to lead me to a woman who was trying to locate her missing husband to have divorce papers served upon him. Another time, I became involved in a case where a wealthy lady had bought an expensive car for a gigolo. She had been wise enough to title the car in her name. She wanted the auto returned. I found the gigolo and the auto. SHE TOOK BOTH BACK!

A similar situation, one that developed into a good continual source, involved a property owner who, along with others in an investment group, owned a large apartment complex and other buildings. One of the partners had passed away and the ad placed was for information about the man's son, who had moved away years before. I found the son and established a long-standing information source.

No information source is too big or too small for your attention. Be consistent and always be on the lookout for new sources. Take time to be intentful and develop a BOOK OF SOURCES for yourself. You may have to only use those sources sporadically over the years, but you will find that when you call, they will remember YOU. The most valuable sources are the BULK creditors, those creditors who have thousands of constantly changing names going through their records. Not only are they good sources of information, but they can often result in becoming large-volume clients for you. Chambers of commerce, business associations, creditor groups and associations, collection agency groups, etc. — all of these and more are constantly having meetings, conventions, seminars, and luncheons. Get on their mailing lists. Join their associations. As a member of the association of commerce, I have gained many opportunities to speak at or be invited to functions where I have met many hundreds of people involved in either collection or law.

I COLLECT BUSINESS CARDS! I hand out my business cards and brochures. You could never remember all of the people you meet at these functions. Carry a notepad and plenty of your business cards. Hand out a short but explanatory brochure about the services you offer. If you are a professional skip tracer and you are invited to be a speaker at one of these affairs, make sure that you not only have a good brochure, but also a number of your SKIP TRACE REQUEST FORMS. If you are a collector involved in skip tracing, you will find that your presence at these affairs will be recognized if you let it be known that your expertise is in skip tracing.

I would like to emphasize again that you should protect your sources of information. Never lend a source to anyone, no matter how much you think it may aid you. Your source will not like it, and I will guarantee it! I have in my book of sources dozens of telephone numbers that take me into source areas not available to many or even anyone at all. I developed these sources over the years by using this *help out* method: you scratch my back and I'll scratch yours. I am a source! I do not mind being listed in anyone's source book. I know this! If you ask for and get my help, I will expect the same from you.

Very close sources of information are your competitors. Stay in touch not only with other skip tracers but also with all of the credit/collection people you are involved with. When searching for a source within a credit collection area, try to gain access to "the person who does your skip tracing." Occasionally I send a list of skips to these people. I receive responses every time, and along with these responses usually come lists of their own skips. I, in turn, will respond to every inquiry that I receive, and I have found that many times when these people request my help in locating skips, they will suggest an amount of renumeration. Oftentimes, professionals in other areas do not have the expertise to do deep, investigative skip tracing nor the time available that it takes and therefore will be glad to employ your help. One of my most consistent clients is an auto repossessor. He is a worthwhile skip tracer, but he has such a volume of business that he does not have the time to actively skip trace. He turns to me and we have established a good working relationship over the years; also, he is a very good source of information.

If you are a professional skip tracer reading this manual, do not think that if you have a yellow page ad in the telephone book you will suddenly start receiving a large number of skip tracing accounts. The term *skip tracing* is peculiar to *our* industry. I have never received a call from my yellow pages ad other than salespeople trying to sell me things. The thousands of skip traces I have received over the years have been gained through my efforts during my source development activities and recommendations from other clients.

Although I have done almost no advertising, the following letter sent to attorneys did bring me several long-term, volume clients. This letter is in reference to the publication for judgment that I mentioned previously. The context of this type of ad will give you information about the subject matter, the name of the plaintiff, the name of the defendant, and the name of the attorney bringing the action. This ad is placed because the attorney has been unable to serve the papers upon the defendant or, in most cases has not been able to locate the defendant for process service (service of legal papers). You have two directions to go in this area.

The Attorney

He knows that even if he is able to obtain judgment through his publication, he must have knowledge of the location of the defendant or his assets if he is to effectively execute the judgment and collect any money. If he is taking his cases on a contingent fee basis, he will surely try everything he can to collect the money or, in the case of repossessable property, get it back. He has to know where the defendant is to perform. This is your in. As he charges on a contingent fee basis, he will expect you to also. I have found that the following letter has been the most effective for communication with these attorneys:

Dear Sir:
In regard to your search for information on the person known as ______________________________. I should be able to locate this person. I have already established some information that may lead me to his current whereabouts. I also may be able to locate his employment and/or assets. Would you consider employing my skip tracing firm for a contingent fee of $ ________? I am enclosing one of my skip tracing request forms for your consideration.

Thank you very much.

Truly Yours,

The Plaintiff

Generally, the plaintiff, confident that his attorney can handle the matter efficiently, will simply refer you to him. However, many creditors have found that there are now too many judgments piled in the files of their attorneys and want to see the money start to come in. They have large investments in these judgments, as they were usually required to pay the filing fees and the publishing costs. They want action, and your call may be able to prompt them into calling the attorney and recommending that he work with you if you are a creditor's collector or hire you if you are a professional skip tracer.

Keep in mind that as I am writing this manual I am referring to both the professional skip tracers and those involved in skip tracing duties at the companies where they work. Not all of you are going to be top-notch skip tracers. Many of you who excel as collectors already know that it is because you are good skip tracers, that you have been able to communicate with more debtors. You may not have the time to devote to skip tracing, or you may simply object to using the methods that are necessary. I hope that, in some way, all of this information will give you a way to resolve these skip trace matters that is, for you, acceptable and efficient. The following list of information sources and now knowing how to develop them into working areas for your purposes should help you to become a more effective skip tracer. I do not think that I would have been able to come along as far as I have without having learned to develop these sources.

PUBLIC INFORMATION SOURCES

Birth Records

Available at county courthouses and often maintained at city halls in smaller communities, birth records give you information concerning the parents of the child, the address at the time of birth, the hospital, and the attending doctor's name. Birth records are also maintained at the state level, usually at the Department of Vital Statistics. This is an essential area for research in developing family histories for family trees, genealogy, and missing heirs. Birth records also can be sources for developing names of parents for skip tracing. In areas where records are kept alphabetically, they can also be used to identify brothers and sisters.

Marriage License Records

Marriage license records are available at county courthouses and can be used to identify the maiden name of a bride, names of witnesses, and ministers or justices of the peace. They also give the address of residence at the time of the marriage. Most applications for marriage ask for other pertinent information such as date of birth, place of birth, names of both parents, and their addresses. This area is also commonly used for the development of family trees, genealogy, and missing heirs. In addition, some state offices maintain these records for the entire state and will give you the lead you need to the county office you need to see the record.

Death Records

Death records are available at county courthouses and are usually kept by an alphabetical file index which gives the date of the passing, the last known address of the deceased, and the file number of the probate record. If you are not able to discern the place of death to obtain this information, the Department of Vital Statistics' records can identify the place of the death.

Probate Records

Probate records are available at county courthouses. A probate file will give you information regarding the estate of the deceased at the time of the hearing. It will give you the name of the estate executor, the creditors, a copy of the death certificate, and other information, including the names of the surviving family members. Often the addresses of the other family members are listed. This record is also essential to family trees, genealogists, and the location of missing heirs. Actual letters to the estate probate executor are kept in this file as well as the final judgment and the disbursement to the heirs.

Divorce Records

Divorce records are located at county courthouses and are also kept in state vital statistics. A record file will be found at the county level and can provide the following information: wife's maiden name; addresses of both parties; attorneys of each party; reason for the divorce action; names of employers or professions; names of creditors, mortgage holders, and banks; names of children and who custody was given to; name of the person custody was given to if not a parent; and information regarding final determination by court as to who receives and who gives. Older divorce records have information regarding motions and petitions made after the final decision for other matters that may have come up such as change in custody and permission to move out of the state.

Adoption Records

Adoption records are found at the county courthouses where adoption took place or at the state level. Until recently, these records have been held confidential even to those who were adopted. Recent rulings have loosened up the stiff restrictions in this area, and you will have to make contact in your area individually to see what criteria have been set for the examination of these records.

Tax Assessor Records

These are found at county courthouses, city halls, or both. Depending on how these records are kept, they can provide you with the name or the names of owners of properties and where the last tax statements were sent to. These records can tell you who previously owned a property and the assessed value.

Building Permits

Building permits are not of too much value to our skip trace efforts. Usually obtained from city hall records, they can provide you with records of home improvements made under permits and the names of the contractors who performed the work. This is a way to confirm the ownership of a property or find co-owners. Contacting a contractor will sometimes gain you a source of other information if the contractor is still collecting from the subject.

Health Department Records

These are city records that control the licensing and investigation of health-endangering complaints. Licenses for businesses have to be obtained from this department. You can establish the name of the owner of a business by checking the name of the individual who requested the permit.

Voter Registrar Records

Generally maintained by the county records, this area allows you to inspect the names and the addresses of the registered voters in a specific area. Some areas will supply you with a computer printout of all registered voters but will charge you for the computer time.

Probation and Parole Records

These records are kept both on a county level and on a state level. You are able to obtain from these records a record of any individual's conviction, term of penalty, release date from probation or from an institution, and the name of the probation or parole officer and his phone number. Obtaining information from the agent is a different matter. Sometimes he will cooperate with you, and sometimes he will try to tell you that the information is confidential and you will have to convince him that it is his job to see that his client lives up to the rules of our society. Do not try to scam this agent. The truth will gain you more cooperation.

Court Records (Civil)

You usually will find these records at the courthouses and maintained by the clerk of courts. Usually filed in alphabetical order by plaintiff or defendant, these records can give you the names of past and current creditors which have sued and are sueing the subject. Often you will be able to finger through the record cards looking at the same last names and find other persons living at the same address or at previous addresses of the subject. Locating older addresses on the debtor will give you the chance to go back into the city directories and identify other members of his family. These records will also provide you with the names of the attorneys who are bringing the suit for the creditor. In the case of a replevin action, they will identify autos and properties held by the subject. Often, you will find a record of a garnishment on an employer or at a financial institution which identifies same.

Secretary of State (Corporate Registration)

Although several states maintain other offices for this area in larger cities within the state, you will usually have to contact the office in the state capital. Information available to you will be concerning the corporate registrations for doing business within the state. It can provide you with the date of the filing, the true name of the corporation, the home place of the corporation, if the corporation is a subsidiary of another company, the names of the corporate officers and their addresses, and the name and address of the corporate agent in the event that it is an out-of-state corporation. If an out-of-state corporation is doing business in your state, it is obligated to register with the Secretary of State's office. Those records will also tell you the condition of the corporation and if it is in good standing. They also record any litigation matter being brought against the corporation.

State Regulation and Licensing

In most states, this area encompasses the professions that are involved with people in areas of finance and health. Some of these areas are the following: doctors, nurses, real estate salespeople and agencies, insurance salespeople and agencies, collectors and agencies, hospitals, clinics, nursing homes, and automobile salespeople and dealers (may be listed in DMV). A call to the general telephone of this area in your state should get you a list of the professions covered. Information available to you from these areas is date and condition of licensing, full name and professional title, address, date of birth, school attended, employer currently licensed to work with (may be more than one), and the owner of the businesses licensed and home address. A record of inquiries from in and out of the state is also maintained, including investigative inquiries, job inquiries, complaints, and lawsuits.

Local Regulation and Licensing

Your local government regulates businesses and individuals in several areas that are important to your work: bar owners, bartenders, taxi drivers and companies, and security guards and companies. Again, a call to your local courthouse or city hall should provide you with information as to what areas are regulated. In effect, the same as maintained by the state regulatories is available here — the subject's name, his address, his date of birth, and the company he is licensed to work for. In some areas of the country, once a license is issued, an individual can change jobs without notifying the regulatory until the renewal date of his license.

SOURCES AVAILABLE TO YOU

Although some of the following source areas are readily available, many of them will have to be developed by you. The information that may be available to you from any of these sources may differ from area to area. You will have to establish for yourself what information is held in any one of these areas, although I will try to describe for each one of them the information I have been able to establish.

Telephone Directory

Here you will find the address and telephone number of subject, same last names at same last known or previous addresses, same last names in neighborhood, relatives, and friends. In smaller communities, you should be able to search the listing for individuals living nearby the last known or previous addresses. Because of the recent changes in the telephone world, information from an operator is now being charged to you. Over a year's period, this can become a big part of your overhead costs, and you should try to avoid it whenever you can.

Information Operator

Listings for your subject could be in his or his wife's name, one of the children's names, an alias that you have discovered, or a relative's name. The information operator now has to give you the address of a listing as well as the phone number. You can confirm the address that you have with the information operator even if the subject has a non-published phone. The reason that she has this information in front of her is to confirm that this is the party that you are inquiring about and not just a "same name" situation. She will not, for any reason, give you the phone number of an unpublished phone. SHE DOES NOT HAVE THE NUMBER! In some major cities in the country, the information operator can put an address into the computer and whatever listings there are at the address appear on her screen. She will only be allowed to give you the number of any same last name listed at the address you have provided. She will not give you any of the other numbers.

Reverse Directories

They are called this because they identify by alphabetical name listing, by address listing, and by telephone number numerical listing. You can obtain from this directory the address of the subject, same last names, and neighbors' listings.

City Directories

Also reverse directories, or commonly called cross-reference directories, they will be able to give you much more pertinent information than basic reverse directories. The most valuable of this information is under the alphabetical category where the names of the individuals are listed. A listing will look something like this: *Smith, John J., (Janet) 1550 Randolph St. Emp. Shucker, Oppies Farm.* Note that they have provided you with the name of the wife, the address, and the name of the employer. Although this information may not be current, it is a lead from which you can develop other clues.

Other information that is provided by this type of directory is a listing for businesses, individually owned and corporate. A business listing will give you the address of the business or other local locations, the manager's name, or the owner's names. The listing for the corporations will usually provide you with the names of several of the corporate officers.

Newspapers

There may be news articles about your subject in various areas, such as arrests and convictions, drunken driving, and general interest. Want ads carry ads that are asking for the whereabouts of individuals, jobs that are available in the profession of your subject, and also things that your subject may be trying to sell.

Credit Bureaus

Credit bureaus maintain records of the credit histories of millions of people from the first time they apply for credit to the most current. This research can provide you with information about a subject's latest recorded address and several of the previous addresses he lived at. It can provide you with the name of his wife, his and her last known employers, and the month and year of their births. The following items are listed on a credit bureau record: credit ratings from open accounts, a record of other accounts although not active, the amount owed at the last reporting, the status of delinquency on accounts as reported by the creditor, inquiries made from creditors and others recently and in the past, judgments filed against the subject, and collections made against the subject by collection agencies. Each time a subject makes an application for credit at a place that subscribes to the credit bureau system, the information provided the creditor is placed on the bureau record whether the credit is given or not.

Credit Reporting Agencies

Independent credit reporting companies are popping up all over the country. They offer and provide an active investigation into a subject's credit and employment history rather than depending on storage records.

Credit Card Companies

It is not too hard to develop a source of information in this area, as credit card companies rely upon outside help for assistance in doing their own locate work. Usually very highly trained collectors, they have always sought out their own sources of information. It is not unusual for them to have established working relationships with the other major credit card companies. Do not contact the head of the department to create your source. He feels that his people are capable and forgets the time when he was a collector and communicated with outsiders. Your source should be one or even more of the collectors themselves. You will find that they will be receptive to your call. Information you will find here will be extensive, and one important thing is that they have the ability to follow a skip through the usage of the credit card.

Department Store Charge Accounts

These are also valuable allies. With the high volume of accounts they have, they keep records on thousands of individuals present and past. Their files are filled with applications. Offering your help on a case that you discover is of interest to a department store will usually get you *in* with at least the collector who is handling the account. If you are good at what you do and are consistent, the collector will spread the news and you will soon have several of the collectors to choose from when you need help.

Department of Social Security

Although you could find virtually every skip you have with the information in these records, establishing a source of information here is nearly an impossible feat. The few times that I have been able to obtain information from this source have been expensive. There is only one way that it will offer any help, and even then it is reluctant to assist you. For a serious, life-related illness, the department will contact the individual and notify him that you are trying to contact him, but it also will tell him the reason.

In the case of a missing heir, I have gotten the department to forward the letter to the last known employer of the heir. It may agree to keep the letter on file until an employer reports on the subject. Unless you can develop an inside contact, you will not ever get this department to give you any information on a skip.

Internal Revenue Service

The Internal Revenue Service is about the same as the Department of Social Security. However, it is easier to find a source within this department. The only information that will be available to the source, of course, is the information on the last filing made by the subject.

State Department of Taxation

This is a little easier than the IRS because it is closer to you. Although it has reviewed certain files for me in missing heir cases, it also only has the information that is reported by the subject.

Insurance Companies

These companies are pretty good at keeping up-to-date on address changes of their insureds. The best sources are in the claims departments. You can usually make a deal with them, and often you will be able to create a new client here. If they are not in communication with the insured for some reason such as a recent accident, they will only be able to provide you with the last known address.

Hospital Records

Unless you are doing some skip tracing or collection work for the hospital, you may not be able to gain access to any of the records.

Sources here are very hard to develop because there are very few people involved in the record keeping department. Your best bet is to communicate with the collection people, although most hospitals only have one or two collection clerks. If you are able to get into this area, the records contain information about the subject, his address and date of birth, and the name of someone to notify.

Doctor's Office Records

These records are accessible to you only if you have inside sources. If you were to find that one of your subjects had gone to a particular doctor and you had no source of information there, your next move would be to contact the collection agency that the doctor uses. It will be able to get information for you if you can establish a relationship with it. Of course, if the doctor's office has reported the subject as a collection account to the credit bureau or as a judgment, you will be able to contact the office directly and cut a deal.

Schools

This area will tell you if the children of your subject are still going to school in your city. If you have a good contact within this area, you will be able to discover the name of the school and the address the child lived at when the school year started. There is no legitimate reason for you to do business with the school board office, so if you are able to make an inside contact, you will have to find a way to do so. A police officer can get any information he wants in this area. He will have to go out of his way to do this for you, so if you have to, only use this source for desperation cases. School boards also maintain records of children who have moved to other cities as records are transferred between them.

Military

In general charts and information in this manual, you will find the information you will need if you ever have to contact one of the military areas for information. Taken through the proper channels, you should be able to locate any person who is in the military or the military reserves. You can also locate your subject through the base locator on the phone if you know the name of the last base he was on.

Post Office

Many people believe that getting information from the post office is near impossible. This is not true. Small town post offices will usually cooperate and give forwardings over the phone. I have found that these smaller offices in the rural areas are a wealth of information. If you can get a postal worker into a conversation about your subject, you can often lead that conversation into a discussion about his relatives in the area. One of the questions I like to ask after I have asked where he has gone is "Where did he come from?" You will be surprised how much the postal workers know. They probably know who he worked for in town and even who his best friend was.

There are three areas of information in a post office that you should be concerned with and a fourth that may help you to locate a business: the forwarding address, the post office box (personal), the post office box (business), or bulk rate permits.

The post office must provide you with a forwarding address if one is available. You may have to go to the post office and fill out a form and pay a fee. It will research the matter while you are waiting. If you cannot get to the post office or it is in another town, you can send a letter on your company letterhead stating your request along with the fee and the post office will respond by mail.

The personal post office box is not as elusive as we think. The post office must, by federal statute, give the inquirer the address of the subscriber if the purpose is for civil process service. The post office maintains a card on all P.O. boxes where the information about the subscriber is kept. If the post office box is that of a company, the post office must provide you with a physical location of that company.

The bulk rate mail section maintains information on companies and individuals that send large amounts of mail at one time and apply for the bulk rate, which is lower than first-class mail. This information should be available to you, but as in all of these areas, if they give you a hard time, simply go to the postmaster and state your purpose.

Newspaper Ads

While reviewing those newspapers for general news and information, you will do yourself good to read all of the want ad section. In doing so, keep in mind the facts you have learned about the skips you are currently working on. Are there ads for jobs in the profession of your skip? If your skip was an employer, is he advertising? If he is one of those people who sells merchandise through the want ads, you may want to contact the numbers that appear. If you know what kind of car he has, he may be trying to sell it to bail himself out of trouble.

Placing "information wanted" ads is a good way of getting leads if you know that the skip has left town, but if he is still in town, your ad may make him hide deeper. Your local newspaper has a library of old newspapers that is available to you for inspection. If someone has given you a lead concerning something that appeared in the paper about your subject, you can go to the newspaper and find the article.

CNA (Telephone Company "Central Names and Addresses")

This is a department of the telephone company that is available to specific telephone personnel, telephone company installers, and linemen. There usually exists one office for each area code, although sometimes more than one area code is handled by a single office. This office, if you are able to locate it and get it to cooperate, can identify the name of the subscriber for any telephone number you have in that area code. You would probably be more successful in the area if you had a source to make the inquiry for you. Whether or not you are able to get an address from this source is now questionable and will depend upon the value of your source. This area does not distinguish between published and nonpublished phones so you may be able to get information for both.

911 (Telephone Company Repair Service)

Information in this area is the same as in CNA, although these people are aware that a phone number is nonpublished. They will not give you the information if the number is so, although they have access to it. Again, you will be more successful in this area by using your source.

DPAC (District Central Information for Service Reps and Installers)

Given an address, this department can supply you with the telephone number listed there even though the number may be a nonpublished one. Again, use your source for this area if you need it.

Banks

Banks can provide you with information on general loan applications, auto loan applications, business loan applications, savings and certificate accounts, and checking account file information cards. It depends on how high up your source is; usually you will have to have a different source for each of these categories unless you are contacting a small town bank. Remember, this is very confidential information, and if you make contact without a inside source, be prepared with a very good *SWAP* or a reason why they should give it to you.

Finance Companies

A finance company is a good source of information that generally maintains applications that are on current debtors, paid debtors, and turn-downs. Finance company collectors are more than often in the beginning of their careers. Their first duty is to learn how to collect. This is a MAKE or BREAK policy that these companies have had for many years. One of every ten succeed in the business, and most of those usually go off into higher-paying credit/collection jobs with more chance for advancement. Those who have made it usually have become very rounded out professionals. Dealing with these starters at the finance company level is pretty easy when you are developing your sources. They are eager to do a good job and will trade information willingly.

Auto industry financing companies are also good sources for the same information, although the personnel are usually more trained and self-reliant. They are usually individuals who have made it though other collection training areas and know the value of your communication.

Credit Unions

These people also have usually received their training in other areas and have progressed to the position because of their experience and fortitude. This area can provide you with the essential information that you will find involved in an application yet will take you even further into the facts because a credit union has the right to communicate with the employer if it is an employer's credit union. Now, many independent credit unions have sprung up all over the country, but I have found that they, too, are receptive and are willing to cooperate.

Associations

Obtain lists of individual memberships and company memberships. Most professional trades have established associations that members stay involved with wherever they go. They usually have paid memberships with annual or quarterly dues and their membership lists are usually current. I have found alumni associations and others like them to be the most valuable sources of information.

Hobbies

Hobbiests are well known to each other. Hobbies like model airplane flying, hot air ballooning, and model train collecting bring these people together often at events and membership clubs. If you have discovered that your subject is an active hobbiest, you may be right on his tail in a very short time if you can locate the clubs he belongs to.

Properties (Physical Examinations)

If you are able to examine a property or an apartment recently left by your subject, you may discover a number of things that can aid you in your search. As mentioned earlier, telephone directories left behind tend to have numbers of friends and relatives written on them along with other notes that may be of interest to you. Things that you should look for are businesses and numbers that have been underlined, and then you should try to establish why. For instance, the number of a doctor or a lawyer may be the clue that you need to locate your skip. The number of a local factory or business may take you to the place where your subject called for a job interview and was hired. Other numbers say different things. Welfare department? Unemployment office? Other things that you may discover on the premises are letters, notes, magazines by subscription, or a pair of size 13 EEE shoes that will tell you that you are looking for a very big person.

Trash Cans

Whether your subject has skipped or not, the contents of your trash can search will almost always give you information about him. Letters, creditors' statements, magazines, empty prescription bottles, and telephone bill toll sheets are some of the things that I feel are the most valuable. Any other information that you are able to find will be a gift for your determination and effort.

Neighbors

Look for those who were close and friendly with your skip. See if they knew anything about him, where he worked or the kind of work he did. Did he drive a company vehicle with the name of the company displayed? Did they notice if a moving company was involved? Did any of the local furniture companies or others make deliveries to him recently? Do they know of any nearby relatives or where the subject was from?

Do they know where he went, or did he talk about moving? What school did his children attend? Did his children have any special friends in the area? There are any number of questions that you can ask of a neighbor. Just because you have gotten what you believe to be sufficient information, do not halt your questioning. Your skip may have left some false clues behind, and when you become aware of it, you will need all of the other information that you were able to obtain. You will also want to check out the neighborhood businesses and the churches.

Churches

Most churches have a set of rules like school districts do. Many times it is required that when a member of a church changes locations, he must register with the new church and records are transferred from the old church to the new one. If members of your skip's family were active in any of the church's functions, they may have made good friends who may be privy to the information that you need.

Magazine Subscriptions

Unless forwarding postage is guaranteed by the shipper, magazines are not forwardable. If you are able to make a contact with the magazine shipper, you may be able to get it to cooperate. The subscriber will often notify the shipper of his new address. The magazine may be that of a trade association the skip belongs to or that of a union. Does he receive a magazine from a specific insurance company that has articles about what the company's agents are doing around the country? He is an insurance salesman and he is licensed to work with that company!

Relatives

If you have been able to discover relatives either from your research or from an application, you will find that amongst them there are answers that will help you, even if they think they know nothing. They will know things like where he is from, where his parents are, who his sisters and brothers are, professions he has been in. One thing leads to another and another and another.

Were you told by one of the relatives that your subject had a death in the family? His father, maybe? Did your listener attend the funeral? Was your skip there? Who else was at the funeral? What funeral home was involved? What city did the father die in? In searching through probate records, you learned that there is information that you could use.

Funeral Homes

Maintain a record of GUESTS who attended the funeral and the name of the cemetery the departed was buried at. The funeral director's records will also reflect the names of the close relatives and their addresses.

Cemeteries

On the register of the persons buried in a cemetery, names and addresses of the relatives who were active in arranging the burial are maintained. This is also a good source of information when you are developing a family tree or searching for a missing heir.

Employers

Employers can supply you with job applications and names of supervisors and friends. The personnel manager will have any correspondence received from other employers the subject is making application to. The payroll manager may have a new address that was given by the skip for the mailing of his earnings statement. This is especially most effective in the months of December, January, February, and March.

Co-workers and Supervisors

These are generally good sources of information. They may be able to provide you with information about your skip's whereabouts from conversations they have had or may give you information concerning the activities your subject was involved in, i.e., softball, bowling league, etc.

References (Given by Debtor to Obtain Credit or Employment)

These are usually very close sources of information that have to be developed from one point to another. One leads to another until you are able to find one in contact or with knowledge that will help you. An experienced loan seeker will usually try to give the credit grantor references that are not family. He will do this for two reasons. The first is that he does not want his close family to be made aware that he is borrowing money, and the second is that he is aware that he is vulnerable and can be found through his family members. Usually, this type has been through the experience and has found out that it was a family member who told. Other references, his friends, are not usually much help at first, but you can prompt their memories as to information that he left in conversations.

Clubs

Clubs that start with "The order of the ____________________" are out. They will not give you any information about their memberships. In fact, they know but little about their members and rarely miss them after they have left. Other clubs, such as in the area of sports, health, and hobbies, are more apt to have information on their members.

Taverns

It is not unusual for a subject to return to his favorite tavern even if he has moved out of the area to the other side of town. He has made friends there and likes the attention he gets by coming in, even if he has to travel across town. He often describes the area he lives in to his friends, trying to see if they are familiar with his new neighborhood. He often tells them where he is working and names some of the new taverns that are in his area. He may be a member of the billiards team or the dart team. The owner of the bar or the other patrons may know of relatives in the area or may have knowledge of where the subject came from.

Grocers

Small or large grocery store, there may be information that will help you. Small grocers, of course, develop friendships with their shoppers and very often know things about the subject. They will even know of other family members who come into the store and can describe where they live. You do not have this personal touch in the larger stores; however, most supermarkets do have check authorization cards on file that can give you information on the subject's bank or his employer.

Paperboy

This little businessman may be able to tell you where the family moved to from conversation he had with them when they cancelled the paper. He may be able to tell you what school the children went to or may have gotten information from the children as to where they were moving to. He may still be their paperboy if their moving away was a planned scam to hide from the creditors, and they may be living in the same house or may have just moved a few blocks away.

Mailing Lists

There are a number of mailing list companies around the country that provide names and addresses for contests and general catalog merchants. These companies purchase their listings from other sales and credit providers around the country. If your subject is around, he sooner or later will appear on one of these lists.

Law Enforcement

This is probably one of the better sources that you will ever establish. Not only do they have extensive records available to them, but they have easy access to records that are either confidential or hard to get. A police officer could walk into a department store, identify himself to the security manager, and get almost unlimited help from the security manager, who would contact the credit department. He has access to police files that you may find very hard to crack.

Collection Agencies

A trade-off source, a collection agency will be very happy to give you any information it has in return for information you may have on someone it is looking for and especially the employment if you have it. The agency may have information from a number of creditors in its files.

Skip Tracers

Whether they are collection tracers or professional skip tracers, this could be a good area for *assists*. They, as you do, want to compile as much information as they can on those individuals who have recently skipped, as they may also get a case in on those individuals. They want to know YOU, too. You are a source of information for them, and you will be placed in their BOOK OF SOURCES. They also have large files and may have already skip traced your debtor.

Investigators

Not necessarily good sources of information, some of them do skip tracing and may have records or will be able to assist you.

Attorneys

An attorney is usually a source of information only on an individual basis. The lawyer is usually hard to deal with, as he finds little time for anything other than his quick, money-making accounts. This is not true of all attorneys, however, and when you do run across those few that seriously work to collect on litigation accounts, you will realize that they are willing to work with you as long as it helps them. In the long run, they can be valuable assets to you as well as you are to them.

Office Supply Stores

They, too, have delinquent accounts to collect. Although the average account is small, they can be a valuable source of information for those commercial matters that you have to resolve. Often, the business that has failed is re-established under another name. The individuals that you are looking for need the credit that office supply stores offer and will try to keep these accounts paid. Contact with the managers of the office supply stores and the help that you can give them on bad accounts will put you in good stead with them for the time that you need them to check their records.

Process Serving Agencies

Agencies of this type have a large number of records to pull from. It is their job to service legal papers on debtors, and often they have to locate the subjects to perform their duties. The information they have on file is the end result of the skip tracers' and the collectors' work, so the addresses that they have are usually the most recent available. A good way to access their records is to create new clients for them from amongst your attorney sources and approach them with your offer of a trade for information when you need it.

Rental and Leasing Companies

These are probably the hardest core collectors you will ever meet. Because of the recent trend to easy credit, they have saturated the market with televisions, stereos, appliances, and furniture. These are rent to own deals, and the easy, no credit check promise attracts all of the credit worms in town. Their losses are great in merchandise although their collection results are very good. Because they have a high number of skips, they are willing to deal with you just about for any reason.

The list of sources is endless. Everytime someone is willing to give out credit, that other someone, the debtor, will be there with his hand out. The list goes on and on. Other areas of information are independent telephone companies, cable TV companies, fire alarm companies, and carbons from computer printouts. If your subject is a painter of houses, he probably has an account at a local paint supply store. If your subject is an electrician, he probably has an account at several of the local wholesale suppliers. So does the roofer. As does the carpenter. Your imagination will create any source that you need.

GO TO IT!

CHAPTER SIX
STORIES I HAVE TOLD

THE CASE OF THE TWO AND ONE-HALF BROTHERS

About two years ago, I became involved in an heir search that was really a true test of my imagination. As it turned out, I was deprived of available information that would have allowed me to resolve the case in just a few days or even less. It was the attitude of an attorney who would not talk about the case unless he was assured that he was going to be paid that made the case so difficult. It took me six months to find the information I needed to solve the matter.

The characters and places in this story are many: a wealthy, elderly woman who passed away without leaving a will; a genealogist; a probate attorney; a family lawyer; a dead doctor; the first wife of the doctor; the second wife of the doctor; two sons from the doctor's first marriage; a third son from his second marriage; a town in northern Michigan; the second husband of the first wife; the second husband of the second wife: a suspicious housekeeper; a luxury apartment in Manhattan; a taxi driver in New York, an airline pilot in Florida; a Nebraska businessman; a car salesman in California; 257 other people; and finally, me.

It all started when I received a call from one of my attorney clients who had received a call from an attorney in northern Michigan. It seemed that a genealogist had contacted him in regard to a doctor who had passed away, requesting information about any children the man had left behind. In an attempt to involve himself in the case, the Michigan attorney took it upon himself to locate the sons he knew the doctor had fathered. He took this action before he received a reply from the probate attorney regarding his inquiry about a fee. When he received the reply, stating that there would be no fee for him, he did not take the time to notify my attorney client that we did not have any authority to continue.

Not knowing this, I proceeded to contact the Michigan attorney, who, for some reason, gave me the impression that the second wife had given birth to two sons, divorced the man, and moved to Pennsylvania. Not only was this not true, but he also gave me the name of the first wife as being that of the second wife. Why he did this, I still don't know, but I must have had my head stuffed into my armpit as I took the information to be real and never bothered to ask any questions about the first wife.

So, I proceeded to look for the wrong woman in the wrong direction. It was several weeks until I realized that I was establishing no leads in this direction. I reviewed my work to that point and realized that I had no more information than I had at the very beginning. I had received answers to all of the correspondence and inquiries I had sent out and had generated nothing. I recalled that the Michigan attorney, who had seemed to be bothered by my call, had ended our conversation by saying that he had given me all of the information that he had and could offer nothing more. His attitude was not one that indicated that he wanted or was even interested in the case, and this bothered me.

I contacted the attorney for the probate, who gave me the number of the genealogist. Upon contacting her, I was informed that I was not officially employed in the matter, and she explained to me that the Michigan lawyer had been told that there could be no fee for him either. She had not been able to locate the sons either, and the only information she had was a mention that the doctor had married a nurse while he was in medical school. She said that she needed to know if he had any children but was unwilling to split fees or compensate me for my help. Technically, I was off the case!

I wasn't going to accept that! I had become involved in the matter and I needed to know the answers. This is me, the way I am. Anyway, I knew that if I was able to locate the children, I could possibly get them to agree to a finder's fee. I had already been told that the deceased had been a very wealthy lady. I did not have any guarantees of a finder's fee, but I had worked on this kind of case before and knew that if the heir had no way of knowing where his good fortune was coming from, he would be likely to sign the fee agreement. Wouldn't you?

Armed with the information that the wife had been a nurse, I decided to start from scratch. I had a working clue. Even though I hadn't located the woman with the name the attorney had given to me and I was still unaware that the information I had been given was confused, I believed that I had the name of the wife. I contacted the Michigan medical regulatory agency that maintains records of doctors and nurses. Sure enough, she had been a registered nurse in the state of Michigan, and the address on record was the same as that of the doctor. I contacted an associate near the area and had him go into the divorce and birth records of the county that the doctor had lived in. As I expected, there were no birth records for any children on file; but to my surprise, there were *two* divorce cases on file! Why the genealogist had not discovered this, I couldn't figure out — other than it may have been the reason that she had contacted the Michigan attorney.

In a few days, I received copies of the files in the mail. The first wife had divorced him because he was an incurable alcoholic, and the file named two sons but only a local address. The attorney representing her was, of course, the one I had contacted FOR BOTH DIVORCES! The second divorce file gave me the name of the other wife and also named a son that had been born of the marriage. Again, only a local address was given for the second wife. She also had been a nurse, and she also had divorced the doctor for reasons related to the use of alcohol. I now had the most important lead I needed to unravel the case and get off in the right direction. I not only had discovered that there had been two wives, but also that there was another heir to be considered. I had the Social Security numbers of the first and second wives. I also had the names of all three sons.

In this manual, you will find a chart of Social Security numbers that can tell you, in almost every situation, where a person is originally from. I took the Social Security numbers to my chart and discovered that the first wife was from Wisconsin and the second wife was from Pennsylvania. The Wisconsin nurse registry indicated that the first wife had registered in Wisconsin, and I was given an address in Milwaukee, although it was pretty old by that time. It became necessary to write to the state of Pennsylvania for the same information concerning the second wife. The reply advised me that she had changed her name upon getting married. I had her new name and a newer address.

I decided to resolve the matter of the second wife first. I had to establish the name of her new husband, which I did by contacting the library in Pittsburgh. I had them go back into the city cross-directory for the year that she had changed her name and found that the name of her new husband was at the address she gave. When I requested that the research clerk at the library come forward, year by year, through the directories, we discovered that just two years later they no longer appeared in the directory. I had the clerk check the suburban directories. No luck. I contacted neighbors and only found a faint memory of them. I called several of the area hospitals until I found the one that she had worked at, and I ran into a brick wall. She had died!

I could only assume now that the son was with the stepfather. Where? I started all over trying to develop a profile of the stepfather. The usual moves gained me very little other than a place where he had worked that was no longer in business. I located the owner of the business, who was unable to tell me anything about the man. He told me that all of the personnel records of the company had been destroyed so there was no application for me to see.

Many states do not respond over the phone to inquiries concerning drivers' records, so I found myself back to letter writing. In addition to the Department of Motor Vehicles, I sent inquiries to the school board, the probate court, the registered property owner of the house where they had lived, the funeral home, and the State Department of Taxation. While I was waiting for replies, I went back to work on the first wife, who had been living in Milwaukee. Milwaukee is my territory. I have little trouble getting information there when I need it, at least I thought so.

She also had remarried. She never did appear in any of the city directories, and I was not able to establish any area of employment for her. I made contact with my source at the school board and learned that both of the sons had attended area schools and both had graduated. I was able to pick up a couple of different addresses that gave me no answers.

I didn't find out about the marriage at first, as the boys' names remained the same through school. It was when I was browsing through my old phone books that I discovered another address under a listing for the eldest son. Cross-indexing the address in the city directory of that year, I discovered that there were two phones listed at that house even though it was a single-family home. I checked the name of the other party and, sure enough, the directory indicated that his wife's name was the same as the first name of the mother.

I checked the current phone book for the man's name and found him listed at the same address even after all of these years. But, it was not to be my day. He listened while I told him why I was calling and then very curtly told me where I could go and hung up. I tried to call him again and he kept hanging up on me. Now, mind you, I had just told him that his stepsons were missing heirs. Knowing that something had to be wrong, I contacted several of the neighbors and shortly knew the whole story. After a very rough marriage, this lady had decided to divorce the man after her boys had gone off on their own. She had moved to Florida. I also discovered that one of the sons had married a girl from the neighborhood. Her parents had moved to California. I was told that both of the sons had moved away and out of state. WHAT IS A FELLOW TO DO?

I had been able to get the birthdates of the two sons from the Michigan divorce records, so I contacted the Wisconsin Department of Motor Vehicles, driver's license records. Son number one had surrendered his license to the state of Wyoming. Son number two had surrendered his license to the state of California. The mother had never had a driver's license under either name. Meanwhile, I received a letter from the State of Pennsylvania Department of Taxation, which indicated that it could not, for any reason, give me information concerning the stepfather of the second son. It very nicely stated that maybe if I contacted the state of New York, where the stepfather was from (according to his Social Security number), I would be able to develop other information.

Just a shot in the dark, as it had worked for me before, I called the information operator in New York City. He was listed! He had a Manhattan address that reeked of wealth. Either this man had inherited a lot of money or he had married money. My second guess was right. Now, I want you to understand that I made this first call with a lot of skepticism. I had run into too many dark alleys in this case to assume that this call was going to be the last one. I called and the person who answered was the housekeeper. She told me that the lady of the house did not take calls from persons she did not know and would not even listen to an explanation as to the purpose of my call. I tried several times over the next several days to get her on the phone and even called asking for the stepfather. No good. She would not cooperate. By now I had come to the point that I would not take "no" for an answer. I sent a telegram. I got no response. I sent a letter to the stepfather and I heard nothing. I then remembered something I had learned while I was in New York years ago. The most respected people in the city are the taxi drivers. It is so hard to get a taxi in New York that many wealthly people have cab drivers on retainer. I made contact with the building management and got the name of the doorman. He told me the name and the number of the lady's cab driver, and I was able to contact him through the company. Now I know that this sounds ridiculous, but New York surprises us with unusual facts. Well, this is one of them. Cab drivers are common carriers of confidential messages in the city. After I told the driver why I was trying to get in touch with her and because he also knew the son (he told me that the son was an airline pilot), he agreed to call the woman and give her my information. Barely ten minutes went by before the phone rang. It was her. She explained to me that she does not take calls because she has been bombarded with calls from charities and others asking for donations. She explained that her husband was still alive but had his own apartment where he spent most of his time. Her son, as she referred to him, was an airline pilot and was based in Florida. She and her husband had adopted him and changed his name. Moreover, she gave me the information I needed to contact him in Florida.

This part of the matter solved, I returned to my search for the other two sons. As I had indicated, I now knew something that made me confident that I was going to locate them. The most obvious route for me to take at this time was to try to contact the son who had moved to the state of Wyoming. Because of the very low population, I have always found it easy to develop early leads in this state and others like it. Information operators in these states usually have all of the states' listings at their fingertips. On the first information call I made, I located a listing for the eldest son. I contacted him and he gave me information which made it possible for me to reach his brother in California and his mother in Florida. When I reached the half brother in Florida, he indicated that his stepfather had told him about his two half brothers and mentioned that he had always wanted to know more about them and where they were. With the permission of the other brothers, I sent him the names and addresses of each of them.

Financially, this whole project turned out to be a losing proposition for me. I knew that when I learned of the adoption of the last son that I probably would not be able to get anything from the finder's fee agreement, although I got him to sign it anyway. In the state of the probate, the law considers adoption to be a waiver of inheritance rights, and my belief was supported when I received a letter from the probate attorney indicating the same. The other brothers declined to sign the finder's fee agreement. I submitted a statement of services to the probate court and I received a check in the amount of $150.00, which amounted to much less than my statement of expenses. However, this was not the first time that I had worked for little or nothing, nor will it be the last. Many of my friends have told me that I am crazy for concluding these matters, knowing that I may not be paid, but I have an undying thirst for winning. I know that every time I resolve a case, I learn more; and when the time comes to use what I have learned, that knowledge will be there. A footnote to this matter of the two and one half brothers: at last count, there were discoveries of over 250 heirs to the lady's estate. Did I really lose anything?

THE SEARCH FOR EDDIE

A lot of the cases that I have worked on could not be resolved in hours or even in days. Many times I have set a case aside when it is making no sense to me. Oftentimes, the facts become jumbled and consistently lead off into the wrong direction. And then, there are those cases that just do not produce clues at the moment I am working on them. So I set them aside. But I set them aside with a plan!

Such was the case in the matter of Eddie. Eddie was a missing heir to an estate of over one million dollars. (Don't you wish!) There are not many cases of this magnitude around, and I was brought into the matter originally as an advisor. You see, Eddie was a missing person that wanted to be missing. He did not want to remain in hiding because he was a bad guy by any interpretation. Eddie just did not like the way his life was being controlled by his parents. Every decision was being made for him. He began to stray away from home. And one day, when he was sixteen years old, he left for good. He left a note that told the family he was fed up with living the life that they had designed for him. The police and many private investigators were not able to locate him and, at the time, they were not able to find a single clue as to where he had gone. The first clue as to his whereabouts came when he was over eighteen years old — he was arrested in Milwaukee on suspicion of burglary. He was released soon after when it was determined that he had not been involved, but this arrest stayed on the record where it was discovered by yet another private investigator. This investigator, employed by Eddie's mother after the death of his father, was not able to locate Eddie in the Milwaukee area. Yes, he knew that Eddie had come to Milwaukee.

Eddie's mother died years later when he would have been approximately twenty-three years old. The bulk of the money he had coming was from her estate. Probate was held without him after another attempt was made to locate him. The money due him was set aside in a fund and remained there gaining interest for the next seven years. It was then that one of his brothers brought an action in the probate court to have him declared legally dead. The judge ordered that the probate attorney make one more attempt to locate him before a decision would be rendered. This is where I was brought into the matter by my friend. As the last and only information about Eddie was the arrest in Milwaukee, the attorney place an ad in our local newspaper, seeking information about him. My friend saw the ad and contacted the attorney.

Eddie was not trying to hide. Had I become involved in this matter four years earlier, I would have found him with one phone call. The problem facing the investigators who had looked was that they did not have sources of information in the Milwaukee area and were apparently not interested in developing any. I have been able to look over their reports since this case was resolved and found that they did very little in the way of investigative work that may have lead to a clue. They did what I call a "surface search." This quick-money, unethical form of investigating is very common. Although many of the investigators around have the knowledge to do a thorough search, many of them will set aside a certain number of hours to earn the amount agreed upon and will not go any further.

The young man that brought this matter to me had done the skim work that all of us learned to do before we initiate a deep search. He did not have a great number of sources to go to so this is where we began in our cooperative efforts to locate Eddie. In the first week, we established the following facts: He had owned no motor vehicles registered in the state of Wisconsin. He had been issued a driver's license that had expired. There was nothing unusual about his driving record that gave us any clues. He had been listed in two of the older city directories that provided us with two different addresses. One of the directory listings indicated that he had been a bartender but did not give the name of an employer. The welfare records told us that he had gotten general assistance and also that he had gone through a job program. Further investigation proved that to be bartenders' school. The county court records indicated that he had a mental health commitment because of a suicide attempt. State records verified the commitment. A recheck of local police files brought no information other than the arrest for suspicion of burglary. Job Service records gave us the name of an employer that he had worked for as temporary help. Other private job services had him on file, but had provided him with no assignments. The rescue mission had given him a place to sleep from time to time. A check of the local credit bureau and the local department stores indicated that he had not applied for credit.

It was time to review. We established the following to be areas for follow-ups: the two addresses that had been in the directories; the listing as a bartender; the bartenders' school; the mental commitment; the temporary job from the state job service; the records at the rescue mission.

We contacted the owners from both of the addresses where he had lived and, although both of them remembered the subject, neither could be of any help. He had been asked to leave from one address because he was living in an apartment that had been rented by a friend of his that moved out when he was unable to pay the rent. We got the friend's name. The other address turned out to be a private home that had been opened up by the owner to roomers. We had to track down the owner's daughter as the owner had died, and she told us that Eddie had been a good tenant, but that one day he just had disappeared. We discovered that it was the same day that he had attempted suicide.

We checked the bartenders' license records. I mentioned earlier that I would have been able to locate Eddie if I had received the case earlier. Matching the dates of the investigator's report to the family, I noted that just two weeks prior to that date he had been issued a bartender's license from the city clerk's office and on his application he had stated the name of his new employer. Upon checking with the owner of the club, we found that Eddie had worked there for over six months. Eddie did not know that his father had died, and had the investigator done a proper job, he could have been found before his mother passed away. Moreover, the bar owner was able to give us the names of two more of Eddie's friends, and we learned that the bartenders' school was no longer in business.

Concerning the mental commitment, we found, upon checking with a source at the county institutions, that Eddie had been committed twice, both times for suicide attempts. We developed a new address from these records.

The temporary job assignment from the state Job Service did not pan out any other information. He had been written off as transient labor and no other record was kept on him.

The only thing that we were able to gain at the rescue mission was a copy of his signature and the name of a place where he had washed dishes. Therefore, we had followed up on all of the leads and found that it was time for another review.

What did we have now?

The name of a friend that he had shared an apartment with.

The names of two friends that he made while bartending.

Another address to check on from the county records — a place where he had washed dishes.

I want you to remember that the principal purpose of our job was to see if Eddie was still alive during the seven years preceding the probate hearing. All of this and more to come did prove that he was alive, and our findings were reported to the probate attorney who set a hearing date. He told us to continue searching.

Although the pieces of information we had developed were few, they were valuable. We now were able to develop a "*profile*" on Eddie and we were beginning to understand his habits. Let's take a look into this profile that we established: We found that Eddie was not hiding. He had only a few select friends. He lived only in low-rent apartments. And he used cash for his needs. The friend he had shared the apartment with was a homosexual. The bar that he worked at was a hangout for homosexuals. Was he? No. Eddie needed to survive during the time that he was under age and apparently became involved with these people even before he turned eighteen years old.

We located each of the three friends (all three instances involved skip tracing) and were able to interview each of them. The first friend had been instrumental in caring for Eddie during the time that he was still a minor. He had even gotten Eddie involved in devil worshipping. The friend did not tell us this information. We got it from the other friend that we located in a city far away from Milwaukee. He gave us enough information to substantiate this statement.

The second friend that we got this information from said that he, too, had been a live-in with the first friend. He admitted that he was a homosexual but said that Eddie was not. He stated that Eddie was just a mixed-up kid that needed someone to help him out. He said that he ran across Eddie one day in the downtown Milwaukee area and spoke to him. Eddie was pretty rundown and seemed to be confused about some of the things this man brought up in the conversation. He had no other information to offer other than that Eddie had told him he had come from a wealthy family and that he wanted no part of it. The friend stated that although Eddie had told his friends many times that his family was wealthy, none of them ever believed him.

The third friend was the worst for us. He apparently had been the closest to Eddie, as friends go, and Eddie had told him, too, that his family was wealthy and that he wanted no part of the wealth or of his family. Right from the start of the conversation, the third friend was evasive in his answers and made it very obvious that he felt that Eddie had the right to be left alone. It wasn't until I told him of the parents' death that he started to cooperate. He said that Eddie had always spoken well of his mother but not so of his father. He felt that Eddie should know that his mother had died. All through the conversation I thought that he was hiding some information that could have helped us. It turned out that he knew nothing at all. We went away with only one thing of any value, yet we did not know at the time that he had received the only positive clue that Eddie had left behind. The friend had said, "Eddie liked horses. Eddie always talked about working on a horse ranch. Eddie said that some day he would like to be in California on a horse ranch." We checked the address that we found on the county records. The owner of this property remembered Eddie but also stated that Eddie had not been a tenant. He had stayed there with a woman tenant. She also told us the woman had also been in the county mental facility and that is where they had met. She gave us the name of the woman.

We were just one block from where Eddie had been a dishwasher so we went there. We found yet another person who had been Eddie's friend and here is where we heard the strangest story. He said that one day when he and Eddie were leaving Eddie's apartment (another address) to go to a ball game, they ran across a man outside of the building that greeted Eddie by his name. Eddie, in turn, introduced the man to his friend as HIS BROTHER! The man told the friend that he had been looking for Eddie for many years and asked Eddie to pack his things and come home with him. Eddie refused. The friend stated that

Eddie told his brother to leave him alone and not to bother him anymore. Then, after a short conversation out of the hearing range of the friend, the brother left. Eddie appeared unaffected by the meeting and went to the ball game with his friend, yet refused to discuss the meeting at all.

The next day, Eddie disappeared from the job and the apartment without taking any of his belongings. This was the very last time that Eddie was spotted in Milwaukee.

We had only one working clue left — the woman that Eddie had lived with. We located her in northern Minnesota. She had no further knowledge of Eddie after the time he lived with her.

Review Time.

Dead stop! We had made all of the right moves. We knew more than anyone had learned about Eddie's life since he left home, yet we had run out of clues. We reviewed the file over and over again looking for something that we had missed.

Recalling the two attempts at suicide, I contacted the coroner's office to see if there were any unidentifieds on record since the last time Eddie had been seen. There were two. One was a body of a black man that had been found in the bottom of a railroad grain car. The other was that of a young white male that had surfaced in the river when construction workers pulled up pilings while building a new bridge. The bridge was four blocks from where Eddie had last lived! The medical examiner's report stated that the body had been lodged between the pilings and could have been in the water for as long as six months. He was unable to establish any approximate date of death. The description of the remains (there weren't many) included that the deceased had had blond hair and and was about the age that Eddie would have been. I tried to track down dental records from the period that Eddie had been in the county institutions, as we had discovered that he had had many problems with his teeth. The dentist that had taken care of the patients at the hospital had passed away and the records were not to be found. Yet, through all of this, I did not know what it was, but I had a feeling about this one. I did NOT believe that this was Eddie.

Although a very weak one, we had come out of this investigation with only one workable lead. Can you remember what it was? What would your next move have been? "Eddie loved horses. He talked about California." Keep in mind that all of the information we were able to develop about Eddie involved facts concerning events that had occurred several years before we were involved. There had been no information that could be related to him since the date of his disappearance. The facts were undeniable! Eddie had either left town or was, in fact, the unidentified body found in the river. Any hope of remuneration for our search beyond the time of the probate hearing which had already been held was in the attorney's promise that he would see that the court would reward us. That was not important at this time. I had committed myself to this case and had decided that I could not quit until it was over, one way or the other.

I decided to put the California matter off until I had exhausted all of the possible moves here in the area that could develop leads. We did, however, mail a letter to the governors of every state, requesting that they search the records of their states in the areas of penal, health, tax and welfare. We eventually received responses from all but six of the states — all very cooperative but with no results.

I sent a letter off to the Department of Social Security, requesting that they forward another enclosed, unsealed letter addressed to Eddie to any current employer they might have knowledge of. I placed ads in all of the local papers, including the shoppers. I contacted a friend who was a reporter with a local television news team. We took an old picture of Eddie, and the station's artist drew a composite of him with the information that we had obtained, and aged him to what we hoped he would currently look like. We had posters made with the composite picture and hung them all over the city. We even took copies of the picture and handed them out at the local taverns that catered to homosexuals. The television station did a feature news item on the air, showing the picture and giving the public a number to call. This prompted several of the local newpapers to contact us for stories that appeared in their papers along with the composite picture.

The calls poured in! You cannot imagine how many people thought they knew Eddie. We interviewed bartenders, drunks, barbers and housewives. Every one wanted to know Eddie. Only one of them really did. We received a call from the owner of a local witch/warlock store who said that he remembered Eddie from several meetings of a group involved in devil worshipping. He named the name of one of the people that we had found to be one of Eddie's friends and we knew that he was being truthful. He described Eddie as being a follower. He said that Eddie "did not belong" in the group and only came because he had been brought by the friend. He gave me the name of a woman (a lesbian) who once told him that she was going to give Eddie a job tending bar for her. And that was all. We had already known about the friend and interviewed him, so we did not pursue that direction any further. I did go over to the woman's bar to speak with her. She confirmed that Eddie had, in fact, tended bar for her for a very short time. He had made no special friendships amongst her customers, but she agreed to ask around and call us if she got any information. She never called.

It was time to set the matter on the shelf. The replies that we had received from the states had not panned out any information. We had sent separate letters to the various departments in the state of California and had discovered nothing. The other work was piling up and I could no longer devote my time to Eddie. I set the file up for a six-month review. I had given over six months of my time to this case and had spent many dollars trying to locate Eddie. Although I reviewed the file several times over the following two years, nothing developed. Then one day I received a phone call that explained why we could not develop any further information after he disappeared. He had somehow made his way to California. We still do not know how or what he did there, but he was found!

Up until this point, Eddie had been known as "John Doe." He had become amnesic and was living in a county home in California. Someday I would take time out to get the whole story, but for now I was just glad that he had been found.

It seems that one day Eddie came out of the amnesic state for just a brief moment and gave his name and his social security number. Remember the letter I sent to the Department of Social Security? The county that was caring for him made a request to the Department of Social Security for possible benefits. There were none, but they forwarded my letter to the institution. My letter described the situation and gave the name of the attorney and the name of the eldest brother. Eddie had indeed been found.

I learned a very important lesson from this case that I have been able to relate to matters that I had previously had since then. Eddie was not hiding. He just did not care, and this is the hardest of all searches.

STORIES THAT I HAVE HEARD

Many of the tales that I have related to you in this manual are probably similar to situations that you have been involved in. Every time I listen to the story of a search done by a speaker, I can relate to any number of my own cases. Each time that I listened, I wondered what direction I would have taken in the speaker's search trying to pick apart his case for a quicker resolution. Often, I have been able to READ BETWEEN HIS LINES; and often, he has surprised me with a method that I would not have thought of. As we go through life in this profession, we always have to keep an open mind. Maybe you could have found a clue that I missed in the search for Eddie. Maybe not.

THE GYPSY RABBITS

I guess that we have all, sometime in our lives, heard stories about the people who wander around in groups, living a carefree life, depending upon only their wit and trickery to survive. Gypsies today are much more sophisticated than they were years ago. This of course is only because we all live in a more sophisticated time.

One of the strangest stories that I have heard involved a group of gypsies travelling through the upper midwest in a caravan of custom vans and luxury cars. Apparently this group did very little other than to travel around the country tricking people and stealing from them. Gypsies are a mysterious people and their whole lives seem to be devoted to con games. Because they hop from place to place so quickly, the teller of this story referred to them as rabbits. He tells of his involvement in this case in such an emotional way that I had to ask him if he was in any way personally involved. He replied that he was.

It seems that the whole matter started when the teller of the story received a call from his older brother, who was the owner of a small motel. Several days before, he was told, a large group of people, who referred to themselves as "entertainers," checked into his motel saying that they would be there for several days. They took ten of the twelve rooms he had available. The unsuspecting brother, happy to fill up his motel, agreed that payment could be made by the "manager" of the group when he arrived in a few days.

The next morning, the entertainers were gone. So was all of the furniture, pictures, radios, television sets and carpeting in all of the ten rooms. Of course, the police were called in to investigate and an all-points bulletin was issued for the thieves. They had gotten away clean. The investigator, the teller of this story, immediately went to his brother's motel. Although the local police were cooperative, they had found out little other than that this same group had been pulling this scam off all over the country and no one was able to catch them. He was also told that the FBI was on the case. In each case, no names were given for the room registry, as the name of the entertainment group was accepted. There were no facts to start with.

Undeterred by this, our storyteller told me that he was determined to solve this case because of the challenge. The motel-owning brother actually gained by the episode because his insurance company agreed to replace all that had been taken and hire his brother to find the thieves. Now, armed with an advance from the insurance company, our storyteller set out to investigate.

His first move was to contact other small-town police departments in the surrounding area to see if the group had hit. With the cooperation of the police chief in his brother's town, he was able to review the reports from around the country and some information received from the FBI. It read like a book. The same group had been working the country for a long time, hitting mostly small towns and moving on. The investigator tried to develop a pattern or a direction of travel from the reports but it seemed that there was no definite highway of travel. Sometimes the group had travelled several hundred miles before hitting. He seemed to be getting nowhere when a report came in about a more recent incident that was identical to other reports around the country. An elderly woman had been scammed and robbed in a small town about two hundred and fifty miles east of the motel caper. The call had come from a police department the investigator had contacted the day before looking for leads. He jumped into his car and drove to the town. When he arrived, he went to see the police chief who took him out to the country home of the lady.

It was one of the oldest tricks of the times. While two young ladies had kept the woman busy in the front yard, someone else went into the back of the house and ransacked the drawers. A good sum of money had been taken. The unusual thing the investigator noted was that even though there were three furnished bedrooms in the house, only one had been searched. Upon questioning the woman, it was discovered that just the day before, two men had stopped by and had identified themselves as county detectives. They had told her that some thieves were in the area robbing homes and asked her to check her house to see if anything was missing, especially cash that she had laying around. Of course, she had gone directly to the room where she kept her cash. She told the two men that nothing was missing and they left, telling her that she could expect a visit from them or the other investigators, two ladies, in the next few days. They had also told her not to talk to anyone about the matter over the phone as it was believed that the thieves got information by tapping the lines.

He and the police chief were about to leave when the phone rang. It was a call for the chief. Another theft report had come in. They responded. The caller to the police chief's office (his house) had told his wife that some apples had been stolen — and not just a few. Someone had picked the lower half of over fifty trees in the back of an orchard. Not only did they take the man's apples, they had taken the baskets to carry them out of his shed. The man showed the police chief from his records that the estimated yield from those trees indicated that over 100 bushels had been taken and maybe as many as 150.

The investigator recruited the help of the chief for an idea that he had. No one was going to eat over a hundred bushels of apples, and if the pattern kept true, the thieves intended to sell the apples. The thieves were apparently going to the east and that meant that they would cross into Wisconsin, or may had already. While the policeman got on the phone and alerted all of the law enforcement offices on the suspected route, including the state police and the FBI, the investigator drove into Wisconsin. Sure enough, a grocer in LaCrosse had purchased fifty bushels from the thieves. The story that they had given him was they had picked the apples. The orchard owner had not been able to pay them so told him they had accepted the apples instead. The investigator knew that he was just hours behind the thieves and that he had to work fast. He drove east on the interstate system, and when he saw a state trooper's car he stopped and told the trooper of his mission. The trooper had seen the caravan several hours before headed in a southeasterly direction, but had observed only six vehicles. He had noticed them only because they had been travelling too close together, but had decided not to stop them. He had not observed any of the license plates. The trooper called in to send word ahead and the investigator continued in the same direction. As he was driving (speeding, he says) he wondered why there had been so few vehicles in the caravan. He checked every exit and every rest stop. The caravan could have travelled many miles ahead of him, and he calculated that if they were staying within the speed limit he was only picking up about ten miles each hour on them, considering the times he slowed down to check the exit areas and the rest stops.

Eventually, he realized that he needed to stop to get gas. As he pulled off of the highway, he noticed a nice-looking late model van parked on the side of the crossroad. The people standing by the van were selling apples! He cruised them and noted down the license plate number. It was a New Jersey plate. He went to the station nearest him and called the state patrol. They said that they would send a car to the sight immediately and also advised him that they had stopped the caravan on the highway about ninety miles south of his location.

All of the gypsies were taken into custody. Information poured in to the law offices and the others were arrested in two groups, one at a motel, the other entering the state of Illinois loaded down with motel furniture that was later identified as that belonging to the investigator's brother's motel. Good job Jerry!

COKE BUST

About a dozen years ago, I owned a collection agency in Kansas City that specialized in the collection of worthless checks. Included in the agency was an investigative service picked up in a merger. The head of this department had a number of interesting stories to tell, the most interesting being the one he referred to as the "soda pop gang." No, he was not telling about drugs. It seems that there was a rash of forged checks being cashed that bore the name of one of the country's major soda companies. Not only were they forged of signature, they were printed, sequentially numbered perfect copies of the real thing. The only difference was that the persons that they were made out to were not employees of the company.

The investigator had not been hired in the matter. He had done some check collecting, and shortly after the checks started to show up in the Kansas City area he began to receive them for collection from his grocer clients. It did not take him long to realize that the checks were complete phonies, as none of the information on them was true. Also forged were the forms of identification being used to pass the checks. Because the checks were being drawn on local banks, they were just returned "no account." It was some time before one of the banks decided to contact the police.

Before the police became involved, the investigator had picked up the challenge. He was already well into his own investigation when he received a visit from the FBI looking for information. Although he had not come upon any pertinent clues yet, the feds agreed to work with him.

The forgers had moved out of the area and reports he got indicated that they were headed eastward. He followed up on every check and gathered all of the information that he could, but came up with no leads. Although he knew that he was not going to be paid for his efforts, he continued to ask questions. When he ran out of places that had sent him checks for collection, he started visiting stores that were not operated by his clients. He knew they were the type of store the forgers had hit. He was amazed at how many of the merchants had just put the checks in the drawer and forgot about them. Not all stores use collection agencies for bad checks, nor even report them to the police. Within just a few days he had located almost a dozen more checks. Only one of them interested him. The number written on the back of the check was a Missouri license plate number. These people were from out of the state, yet why a Missouri plate?

He ran down the plate and found that it was issued to a woman in Kansas City. When he went to the address he found that she had moved several months earlier. He noted that the date of her move coincided with the dates of the earliest checks written. He wondered what he was headed for. Had the forgers recruited a local? His next move was to locate the woman. He had received information from the landlord of her old address that directed him to her employer. She no longer worked there and the employer had expressed to the investigator that her quitting had come as a surprise to him. Had she left town with the gang?

Before she had left, she had mentioned to one of the other girls in the office that she had a new boyfriend — a wealthy man who lived in one of the area's most expensive apartment complexes — and that she was moving in with him. Even the investigator was familiar with the units she had mentioned. And the office girl not only confirmed it, she had a phone number that the woman had given her. Was this luck or just good sound investigating? This was the first solid lead ever picked up on the gang in all of the police and federal involvement.

He wondered if he should continue on his own or contact the agent (FBI) that had left him involved. He decided to continue. A visit to the apartment complex gained him his first big clue. Although the woman had been asked to leave when the rent had not been paid, the manager of the complex was able to provide him with the license plate numbers of the cars that had been authorized to park in the complex's assigned slots. He also gave the investigator the name of the man with whom the woman had been living. The name turned out to be one of the phoney names that had appeared on the forged checks. The license plate had been issued in Florida. The big surprise was yet to come. The manager was holding the mail that had come to the gang member. One of the pieces of mail was a very thick phone company billing envelope.

It was time to call on the agent's help. When the fed arrived, the manager surrendered the mail to him. Inside were long-distance toll sheets listing dozens of calls to Florida, numbers in Nevada, New Mexico and, most recently, calls to St. Louis.

It all stacked up like this: the calls to Nevada were to a hotel where the ringleader had stayed; the calls to New Mexico were to numbers that had been disconnected but turned out to be numbers that had been listed to other gang members; the Florida calls were to a print shop owned by a member of the gang; other Florida calls were to the unlisted number at the home of the ringleader; and the calls to St. Louis led the federal investigators to an apartment where the gang was staying while they were waiting for a new supply of checks to come from Florida.

This forgery ring had been one of the country's longest surviving operations. If it had not been for the hard work of the investigator, how long would they have lasted?

I could go on for days telling you these stories. The next time that you are involved in a conversation with a skip tracer or a collector, ask him this question: "What was your most unusual case?" You might have to gag him to shut him up. We have all had some stories to tell, but if you have not, YOU WILL!

CHAPTER SEVEN
GENERAL CHARTS AND INFORMATION

I have often wondered how I could describe the assimilation of the information that goes through my mind. As one clue compounds another, we find we are actually in the business of dissolving clues rather than of resolving them. This may sound strange at this point, but we cannot move from clue to clue until we disprove the preceding one. A clue that is not completely dissolved is still a workable lead. Therefore, it becomes imperative that we tolerate each clue until it's totally dissolved. If we do not, we lost the context of the clue and of the information within.

Let me give you an example. Imagine yourself driving up to an intersection where several unmarked roads cross. This intersection is your first clue. You have to decide which direction you are going to travel from that clue, keeping in mind that there still remains two other directions you could have chosen. You say to yourself that if the first direction you took does not resolve your quest, you can always return to the intersection and take another direction, and so on. What happens if the road you are on takes you to another intersection and you are faced with several other directions to travel? Accordingly, this may happen to you several more times, and when you arrive at one of these distant intersections (clue) you suddenly find that you have come to a dead-end road and the only way to travel is back. Can you find your way back to the first intersection? Did new discoveries, even though eventually dissolved, cloud the importance of the direction at the first intersection? Or did you just forget about the other two directions?

Suppose that your mind is a pyramid built of triangles. Every pyramid has its pinnacle, and each pinnacle, a triangle, representing the first building block of your pyramid Thus, you have:

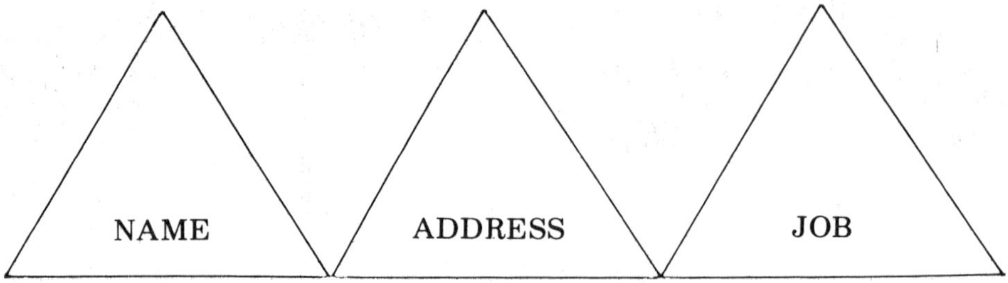

Each of these triangles represents the first clue in every direction you have available to you at the first intersection. Each is a basic building block for a new pyramid of progressive clues. Your pyramid begins to take shape:

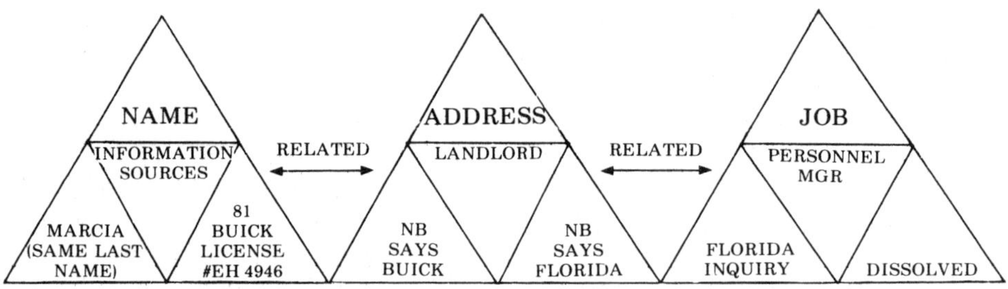

Note that you have created a second line of offense. However, you have done so without losing sight of the first intersection. Now you must review your second line of offense. You are looking for two things: progressive moves and related matters. The progressive moves you find are those directions that have not dissolved. To dissolve, you have no further direction, nor have you found any relationship to other clues. Your direction is *not* dissolved if you note a relationship to another direction. A statement from two or more directions strengthens your clue.

Your second line of offense has brought you several bits of information, including the dissolution of the landlord and the personnel manager. If you have reviewed your first clue thoroughly through your information sources, you can now dissolve it too. Do not progress from any offensive level until you have gained all of the information available. Note that you have created five more clues and one dissolution in your third offensive line. Among these clues are two relationships and one undissolved clue.

You must now review your file. You have only one person in the area with the same last name. DMV indicates that your subject drives a 1981 Buick, license number EH 4946. A neighbor confirms that he drove a similar car. Another neighbor says that your subject may have moved to Florida. The personnel manager at his old job received an inquiry from a job contact in Florida.

YOU HAVE *THREE* NEW PINNACLES (Starting Blocks)

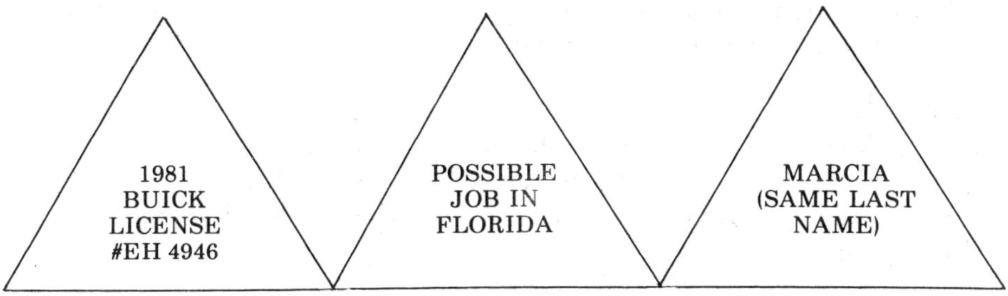

If you have asked all of the questions you should have you may have gotten much more information than what is shown here. For instance, during your DMV inquiry you may have found that there is a lienholder on the Buick. They have information about your subject. You could have found that the auto plates were due to be renewed shortly or that they had just been renewed to a more recent address. The personnel manager may have saved the letter he received and given you the name of the inquiring employer in Florida. Any other information that you developed also becomes a new pinnacle — a new beginning.

LETTER WRITING

In many cases, you will find that sources of information will not respond to your inquiry over the telephone. You will have to correspond through the mails to get the answers that you need and then, unless you are able to generate a reason for the reader to give you those answers, you may just have wasted the postage. People in numerous areas have taken the attitude that they just don't want to violate consumer laws (even if they do not understand them) and will refuse to answer your inquiries. If they do answer, what you will receive is a short note stating that they hold policy that prevents them from disclosing any information. This is why, if you do not have a legitimate cause, your letters must say *nothing* about the reason for which you want the information. If you are looking for a missing heir or the beneficiary of an insurance policy, if you are an employer offering a job to the subject or a doctor trying to inform the subject that he has been exposed to a dangerous germ, then yes, you have a legitimate reason for your inquiry that may bring a reply. If you are looking for your subject to collect a delinquent account or to repossess his car and you disclose this information, you not only will get no reply, you may have made yourself liable if this information is passed on in anyway which causes harm to the subject.

I have found the following letter to be the most effective when writing to areas where the decision to reply is optional.

Dear Sirs:
It is imperative that we learn the current whereabouts of ________ ____________________. If you have any records that may help us locate him, we would be grateful for your cooperation. Will you please check your ____.

Truly yours,

Note that this is an open letter form and can be used to inquire at various information sources areas. For instance, if this letter were going to a last-known or previous employer, you could complete the third sentence as follows: "Will you please check your copy of his employment application for information concerning any relatives or friends listed?" If there is other information that you know will be available on the application, such as his date of birth, Social Security number or middle initial, you can add these items to your sentence.

This letter only implies that you have a want for the information and gives the reader no reason for determining the value of your request. I have also found that your letterhead must not contain information that will disclose your purpose for the inquiry. If you write this type of letter with the letterhead "JOHN C COLLECTION AGENCY," you will have defeated the purpose of the letter. Your letter should not be on plain paper, either, but for legitimacy should have a business format. The initials JCCA (JOHN C COLLECTION AGENCY) imply nothing that will create suspicion. The following letters are those that I have found to be the most effective over the years. Each contains the impetus for the disclosure of the information and the information necessary for the reader to identify the subject of the inquiry. After each letter you will find a list of areas that you can write to when using that letter.

Searching the Military:

Dear Sirs:
We are attempting to locate the following individual, whom we believe is a member of your branch of the service. The following information is available for your search.

Full name ______________________________

Social Security no. ______________________________

Date of birth______________________________

Place of origination______________________________

Please reply as to the current whereabouts of this person. We enclose a self-addressed stamped envelope for your convenience. This request is urgent.

Truly yours,

The target of this letter is one or all of the following:

ARMY—Officer Personnel on Active Duty

The Adjutant General
Department of the Army
Attention: AGPF-FC
Washington, DC 20310

ARMY—Enlisted Personnel on Active Duty

Commanding Officer
U.S. Army Personnel Services Support Center
Attention: AGPF-V1
Fort Benjamin Harrison, IN 46216

ARMY—Enlisted and Officer Personnel
Not on Active Duty

Commanding Officer
U.S. Army Administrative Center
9700 Page Blvd.
St. Louis, MO 63132

AIR FORCE

Directorate of Administrative Services
Department of the Air Force
Attention: Military Personnel Records Division
Randolph Air Force Base, TX 78148

NAVY

Chief of Naval Personnel
Department of the Navy
Washington, DC 20370

MARINE CORPS

Commander of the Marine Corps (Code DGK-7)
Headquarters U.S. Marine Corps
Washington, DC 20380

COAST GUARD—Enlisted Personnel

Commandant (PE-3)
U.S. Coast Guard
1300 E. Street, NW
Washington, DC 20591

COAST GUARD—Officer Personnel

Commandant (P.O.)
1300 E. Street, NW
Washington, DC 20591

The above offices of the military will be very reluctant to assist you in your search if you do not provide them with the proper information. As mentioned earlier in this manual, if you know where the individual was last stationed, the base locator should have access to transfer information.

Searching Government Records:

Dear Sirs:
It is our urgent request that you search your records for information that may lead us to the current whereabouts of

Full name ____

Date of birth _______________________________________

Social Security No. ___________________________________

We have exhausted all general sources of information regarding our search for this individual and it is our wish that you give us any information you have so we can contact him regarding ________________

____

Truly yours,

Do not try to deceive the government and give them a false reason as to why you want to contact your subject. If you are dealing with a public information area, they will supply you with whatever information that can be available to you. Generally, however, they do ask you for a reason and what this information is to be used for. As noted earlier in this manual, the beginnings of your search should be in the local records areas where you can usually make your request by telephone. This type of request letter should be used locally only if it is required, and to the state records when necessary.

A vast number of records are available to you through your use of the proper channels. The following list of government offices and their addresses will help you search the categories of births, deaths, marriages, state institutions (including medical and mental), probation and parole, and prisons. Here they are listed in alphabetical order by state: (Fee is required)

Alabama
State Dept. of Public Health
Montgomery, AL 36130

Alaska
Dept. of Health and Welfare
Pouch H
Juneau, AK 99801

Arizona
State Dept. of Health
P.O. Box 3887
Phoenix, AZ 85030

Arkansas
State Dept. of Health
Little Rock, AR 72201

California
State Dept. of Public Health
410 N. Street
Sacramento, CA 95814

Connecticut
State Dept. of Health
79 Elm Street
Hartford, CT 06115

Colorado
Colorado Dept. of Health
Denver, CO 80220

Delaware
State Dept. of Health and Social Services
Dover, DE 19901

District of Columbia
D.C. Dept. of Human Resources
Vital Records Section
Washington, DC 20004

Florida
State Division of Health
P.O. Box 210
Jacksonville, FL 32201

Georgia
Dept. of Human Resources
Vital Records Section
Atlanta, GA 30334

Hawaii
State Dept. of Health
P.O. Box 3378
Honolulu, HI 96801

Idaho
Bureau of Vital Statistics
Statehouse
Boise, ID 83720

Illinois
State Dept. of Public Health
Springfield, IL 62761

Indiana
State Board of Health
Indianapolis, IN 46206

Iowa
State Dept. of Health
Des Moines, IA 50319

Kansas
Bureau of Registration and Health
Topeka, KS 66620

Kentucky
Dept. of Human Resources, Vital Statistics
275 Main Street
Frankfort, KY 40621

Louisiana
Office of Vital Records
P.O. Box 60630
New Orleans, LA 70160

Maine
State Dept. of Health and Welfare
Augusta, ME 04333

Maryland
State Dept. of Health and Mental Hygiene
Baltimore, MD 21203

Massachusetts
Registrar of Vital Statistics
Boston, MA 02108

Michigan
Office of Vital and Health Services
Lansing, MI 48914

Minnesota
State Dept. of Health
Minneapolis, MN 55440

Mississippi
State Board of Health
Jackson, MS 39205

Missouri
State Dept. of Public Health and Welfare
Jefferson City, MO 65101

Montana
State Dept. of Health
Helena, MT 59601

Nebraska
State Dept. of Health
Lincoln, NE 68509

Nevada
Dept. of Human Resources
Carson City, NV 89710

New Hampshire
Bureau of Vital Statistics
61 South Spring Street
Concord, NH 03301

New Jersey
State Dept. of Health
Trenton, NJ 08625

New Mexico
New Mexico Health and Social Services Dept.
Santa Fe, NM 87503

New York
State Dept. of Health
Albany, NY 12237

New York City
Dept. of Health of New York City
New York City, NY 10013

North Carolina
State Board of Health
P.O. Box 2091
Raleigh, NC 27602

North Dakota
Division of Vital Records
Bismarck, ND 58505

Ohio
State Dept. of Health
Columbus, OH 43215

Oklahoma
State Dept. of Health
P.O. Box 53551
Oklahoma City, OK 73105

Oregon
State Board of Health
Portland, OR 97207

Pennsylvania
State Dept. of Health
New Castle, PA 16103

Rhode Island
State Dept. of Health
Providence, RI 02908

South Carolina
State Dept. of Health
Columbus, OH 29203

South Dakota
State Dept. of Health
Pierre, SD 57501

Tennessee
State Dept. of Public Health
Nashville, TN 37219

Texas
State Dept. of Health
Austin, TX 78701

Utah
Utah State Dept. of Health
Salt Lake City, UT 84110

Vermont
Public Health Statistics Division
Dept. of Health
Burlington, VT 05401

Virginia
Dept. of Health
Richmond, VA 23208

Washington
Vital Records
P.O. Box 9709
Olympia, WA 98504

West Virginia
State Dept. of Health
Charleston, WV 25305

Wisconsin
Division of Health
Madison, WI 53701

Wyoming
Wyoming Division of Health and Medical Services
Cheyenne, WY 82002

NOTE: Adoption records are only released to those individuals they pertain to and are in no way exposed to the general public. Moreover, not all states maintain records on penal institutions and probation and parole in this department; therefore, when you contact them for the amount of the inquiry fee, check with them on this if it applies to your case.

SOCIAL SECURITY STATE IDENTIFICATION

The first three numbers of the Social Security number, in most cases, will identify the state in which your subject originated. Most of us are assigned our Social Security numbers at a time in our teens.

001-003 New Hampshire
004-007 Maine
008-009 Vermont
010-034 Massachusetts
035-039 Rhode Island
040-049 Connecticut
050-134 New York
135-258 New Jersey
259-211 Pennsylvania
212-220 Maryland
221-222 Delaware
223-231 Virginia
232-236 West Virginia
237-246 North Carolina
247-251 South Carolina
252-260 Georgia
261-267 Florida
268-302 Ohio
303-317 Indiana
318-361 Illinois
362-389 Michigan
390-399 Wisconsin
425-428 Mississippi (also 587)
429-432 Arkansas
433-439 Louisiana
440-448 Oklahoma
449-467 Texas
468-477 Minnesota
478-485 Iowa
486-500 Missouri
501-502 North Dakota
503-504 South Dakota
505-508 Nebraska
509-515 Kansas
516-517 Montana
518-519 Idaho
520 Wyoming
521-524 Colorado
525 New Mexico (also 585)
526-527 Arizona
528-529 Utah
530 Nevada
531-539 Washington
545-573 California

400-407 Kentucky
408-415 Tennessee
416-424 Alabama
574 Alaska
575-576 Hawaii
577-579 District of Columbia

STATE MOTOR VEHICLE INQUIRIES

Because of control by the state government, you will have to show a legitimate reason for your need of information about motor vehicles. Several states offer "open accounts" for those who consistently need this service. As there is usually a basic monthly fee required, it is suggested that unless you inquire in volume numbers to any particular state, you make your inquiries on a per time basis, by mail. You will have to contact each office (in each state) before your inquiry to learn the requirements and the amount of the fee required.

Dear Sirs:
It has become necessary to contact you in our effort to locate the following person for the purpose of ______________________
Full name ______________________ Date of birth ________
Last known address ______________________
Driver's license no. ______________________
City ______________________ State __________ Zip__________

We are aware of his/her ownership of the following vehicles:

Year	Make	ID#	Plate#

Please check your records in the areas indicated above for pertinent information.

Truly yours,

I have found that asking too much in this letter brings only a brief return. Yet, because there is other information in their files, I usually attach a second "NOTE" to the letter, which reads as follows:

If the vehicles mentioned have been sold, will you please indicate the name and the address of the new owner? I would also appreciate it if you can check the following records for information on the subject that may be of help to me:

Lien holders

Co-owners

Safety and Responsibility

Thank you.

This method seems to bring more information when you separate it as I have done here. Remember, there are several departments within the motor vehicle department that maintain the information you require. If an individual state requires a separate request for each department, you will have to comply. Do not try to shortchange them.

The following listing for the various departments of motor vehicles should give you quick reference to enable you to locate the correct information you will need to correspond with a particular department. You will have to call for the fee required and the direct address.

Department of Transportation

ALABAMA	501 Dexter Ave.	Montgomery 36104	205-832-3327
ALASKA	338 Danalie St.	Anchorage 99501	907-279-1451
ARIZONA	206 17th Ave.	Phoenix 85007	602-261-7226
ARKANSAS	P.O. Box 1272	Little Rock 72203	501-371-1341
CALIFORNIA	1120 N St.	Sacramento 95814	916-445-2201
COLORADO	4201 Arkansas Ave.	Denver 80210	303-757-9201
CONNECTICUT	24 Wolcott Hill Rd.	Wethersfield 06109	203-566-3477
DELAWARE	P.O. Box 778	Dover 19901	302-736-4306
DIST. OF COLUMBIA	301 C. St.	Washington 20005	
FLORIDA	605 Suwanne St.	Tallahassee 32301	904-488-6721
GEORGIA	2 Capitol Square	Atlanta 30334	404-656-6000
HAWAII	869 Punchbowl St.	Honolulu 96813	808-548-3205
IDAHO	3311 W. State St.	Boise 83702	208-334-3887
ILLINOIS	Administration Bldg.	Springfield 62764	217-782-5597
INDIANA	State Office Bldg.	Indianapolis 46204	317-232-1470
IOWA	800 Lincoln Way	Ames 50010	515-239-1101
KANSAS	State Office Bldg.	Topeka 66612	913-296-3461
KENTUCKY	State Office Bldg.	Frankfort 40601	502-564-4890
LOUISIANA	P.O. Box 94245	Baton Rouge 70804	504-342-7501
MAINE	State House #16	Augusta 04333	207-289-2551
MARYLAND	P.O. Box 8755 BWI	Baltimore 21240	301-859-7397
MASSACHUSETTS	1 Ashburton Place	Boston 02108	617-727-7680
MICHIGAN	P.O. Box 30050	Lansing 48909	517-373-2114
MINNESOTA	Transportation Bldg.	St. Paul 55155	612-296-3000
MISSISSIPPI	510 George St.	Jackson 39202	601-961-4733
MISSOURI	P.O. Box 270	Jefferson City 65102	314-751-4622
MONTANA	1424 9th Ave.	Helena 59601	406-449-3423
NEBRASKA	P.O. Box 94799 S.	Lincoln 68509	402-473-4615
NEVADA	1263 So. Stewart St.	Carson City 89710	702-885-5440

Department of Transportation

NEW HAMPSHIRE	P.O. Box 483	Concord 03301	603-271-3734
NEW JERSEY	1035 Parkway Ave. CN600	Trenton 08625	609-292-3535
NEW MEXICO	P.O. Box 1028	Santa Fe 87501	505-827-4651
NEW YORK	Campus Bldg. #4	Albany 12232	518-457-4422
NORTH CAROLINA	1 So. Wilmington St.	Raleigh 27611	919-733-2520
NORTH DAKOTA	Capital Grounds	Bismarck 58505	701-224-2513
OHIO	25 So. Front St.	Columbus 43215	614-466-2335
OKLAHOMA	200 N.E. 21st St.	Oklahoma City 73105	405-521-2631
OREGON	135 Trans. Bldg.	Salem 97310	503-378-6388
PENNSYLVANIA	1200 Trans. Bldg.	Harrisburg 17120	717-787-5574
RHODE ISLAND	State Office Bldg.	Providence 02903	401-277-2481
SOUTH CAROLINA	955 Park St.	Columbia 29202	803-758-2716
SOUTH DAKOTA	Trans. Bldg.	Pierre 57501	605-773-3265
TENNESSEE	#700 Polk Bldg.	Nashville 37219	615-741-2848
TEXAS	11th and Brazos	Austin 78701	512-475-8044
UTAH	4501 S. 2700 W.	Salt Lake City 84119	801-965-4113
VERMONT	Administration Bldg.	Montpelier 05602	802-828-2657
VIRGINIA	9th St. Office Bldg.	Richmond 23219	804-786-7639
WASHINGTON	Hwy, Admin. Bldg.	Olympia 98504	206-753-6054
WEST VIRGINIA	1800 E. Washington St.	Charleston 25305	304-248-3259
WISCONSIN	4802 Sheboygan Ave.	Madison 53705	608-266-3666
WYOMING	2200 Carey Ave.	Cheyenne 82001	307-777-5266

It is important that you realize addresses change often within the state areas. To the best of our knowledge, the addresses above are the latest used by this office. Therefore, it would be wise if you made a telephone contact before sending mail. It is also interesting to note that several states still give information from their motor vehicle records over the telephone without charge.

I cautioned you earlier in this manual about disclosing any of your sources of information to others. To show you what can happen, look at this case. Up until about nine years ago, Wisconsin was a state that would give information to anyone over the phone at no charge. At that time, not many were aware of this and we had a free hand with the DMV. Someone let the word out to a major credit card company, they in turn disclosed it to a department store collection staff, and the calls began to flood in to the DMV. Because of this, they were forced to set up accounts and begin charging for the information. I do not disagree with this policy, however, as the privilege was being misued. PROTECT YOUR SOURCES, AT ALL COSTS!

As I said, protect yourself and, in doing so, protect your resources. ARE YOU RESOURCEFUL? Do you make up good stories? Can you tell a story that is harmless to all in such a way that you will convince your listener that you are who you want him to think you are without telling him who you want to be? In other words, can you convince someone that you are a person who has a need for information that they have been told not to give to anyone, REGARDLESS!? Look at this example. "Hello? My name is Billy Buckle and I used to live with my brother Tom Buckle at 0000 So. 10th St. I wonder if you can help me. Tom moved away without paying some bills but he has sent me some money and a note to call you to see how much he owes. Part of the bill is mine, I guess, and I'll pay for the long distance calls. Can you send me a copy of the unpaid bill and the record of the long distance calls?" WHO DID I JUST CALL? WILL I GET AN APPROPRIATE REPLY? YES, I WILL! I will be asked what the number was for billing, and they will look at the billing and ask me where to send the copies.

See what you can do with these words:

I am the accountant for . . . .

I represent . . . .

He was issued the wrong . . . .

My publisher says that I should not tell you to lie. I will respect their opinion and tell you only this: I have done hours of research on laws governing lying. I have found only these consequences.

1) You cannot say you are or in any way identify yourself as a government official.

2) You cannot say you are or in any way identify yourself as a utility company employee.

3) You cannot say anything about anyone that will impugn, defame or imply that his character is less than what it is publicly known to be. There are no other definitive laws on the books that provide penalty for lying outside of these categories. All areas of law enforcement use *white lies* to gain information and resort to *trickery* to catch the bad guys. I will too! "Hi! This is Billy Buckle. Where have you been sending my ______________________________?"

SKIP TRACE WORKSHEET

I have emphasized the importance of a good working field — a solid format for the information that you have and will develop. The pyramid I showed you earlier illustrated what I believe to be the most effective way of THINKING out a skip trace. The following skip trace worksheet is a hands-on record of information that you will compile on your subject. I still use this format on all of the tracing work I do. All of the information that I originally receive is transferred to this sheet so that I can better assimilate it and take direction. I have used this format in all of the training sessions I have held and have found it to be the most comprehensive for the student. With a little imagination and hard work you can join the ranks of those who have worked with me in the past. In the following order they have become: a credit manager for a national paid manufacturing company, a vice president of a credit card company, a collection agency owner and the owner of a rental store chain.

SKIP TRACE WORKSHEET

NAME ____________________________________ 1 2 3

SPOUSE OR OTHER ____________________________ 1 2 3

ADDRESS __________________________________ 1 2 3

CITY _______________ STATE ________ ZIP ________ 1 2 3

PHONE ________ IN WHAT NAME? ________________ 1 2 3

ALIASES __________________________________ 1 2 3

PROPERTY OWNER ____________________________ 1 2 3

REALTY COMPANY ____________________________ 1 2 3

MORTGAGE COMPANY __________________________ 1 2 3

RENTAL MANAGEMENT AGENCY __________________ 1 2 3

CHILDRENS' NAMES ___________________________ 1 2 3

SCHOOL ___________________________________ 1 2 3

PLACE OF EMPLOYMENT ______________________ 1 2 3

ACTIVE? _______ TERMINATED? _______ HOURS? _______

WAGES? _______ DEPT? _______ 1 2 3

SUPERVISOR'S NAME ______________________________

DIRECT PHONE ______________________________ 1 2 3

SPOUSE'S EMPLOYMENT ______________________________ 1 2 3

NEIGHBORS ______________________________ 1 2 3

______________________________ 1 2 3

______________________________ 1 2 3

______________________________ 1 2 3

FRIENDS AND REFERENCES

______________________________ 1 2 3

______________________________ 1 2 3

______________________________ 1 2 3

______________________________ 1 2 3

1— confirmed information 2— made contact 3— resolved all clues

CREDIT INFORMATION

Open Accounts ______________________________ 1 2 3

______________________________ 1 2 3

______________________________ 1 2 3

______________________________ 1 2 3

______________________________ 1 2 3

______________________________ 1 2 3

______________________________ 1 2 3

Closed Accounts ______________________________ 1 2 3

______________________________ 1 2 3

______________________________ 1 2 3

______________________________ 1 2 3

______________________________ 1 2 3

______________________________ 1 2 3

Banking	______________________	1 2 3
	______________________	1 2 3
	______________________	1 2 3
Credit Record	____________ Rating ______	1 2 3
	____________ Rating ______	1 2 3
	____________ Rating ______	1 2 3
	____________ Rating ______	1 2 3
	____________ Rating ______	1 2 3
	____________ Rating ______	1 2 3
Inquiries	______________________	1 2 3
	______________________	1 2 3
	______________________	1 2 3
	______________________	1 2 3
	______________________	1 2 3
Judgments	______________________	1 2 3
	______________________	1 2 3
	______________________	1 2 3
	______________________	1 2 3
	______________________	1 2 3

Notes:

Other Credit Discoveries

____ 1 2 3

____ 1 2 3

____ 1 2 3

____ 1 2 3

____ 1 2 3

____ 1 2 3

____ 1 2 3

Notes:

MOTOR VEHICLE INFORMATION

MAKE ________ TYPE ________ VIN ________________ 1 2 3

LICENSE NO. ____________ STATE _____ COLOR _____ 1 2 3

MAKE ________ TYPE ________ VIN ________________ 1 2 3

LICENSE NO. ____________ STATE _____ COLOR _____ 1 2 3

TITLE NUMBER 1 ____________________________ 1 2 3

TITLE NUMBER 2 ______________________________ 1 2 3

OTHER INFORMATION DISCOVERED DMV

______________________________ 1 2 3

______________________________ 1 2 3

______________________________ 1 2 3

______________________________ 1 2 3

______________________________ 1 2 3

DRIVER'S LICENSE RECORD D.L. NUMBER ________ 1 2 3

______________________________ 1 2 3

______________________________ 1 2 3

______________________________ 1 2 3

______________________________ 1 2 3

______________________________ 1 2 3

______________________________ 1 2 3

Note that at the end of each line, the codes "1, 2, 3" appear. The purpose of the codes are to keep you informed about the level of activity you have reached on each line. I, for one, can testify to a poor memory when my head becomes cluttered with several cases at a time. There have been times when I have forgotten to address these codes and found myself duplicating procedure just to find out that I had done it already.

Failing to keep notes (stapled to your file) is your quickest way to failure. Many times we will have to set aside cases for future follow-ups. The information that you have developed can be lost or forgotten in just a few days if you do not have a reliable reminder system. I have a very simple one — A CALENDAR! Each time I discover a fact or event that is to take place on a future date, I place that information on my calender whether or not I am close to resolving the case. The day will arrive that I have to review the file and my calender will remind me. If I have resolved the case, it simply will not be in my working file.

You must also watch out for information decay. A lead that is good today may be worthless tomorrow. I recall a case where one of my employees received information that a subject's wife had come into the city to visit her parents. He had also been informed that she had driven into town and was driving her mother around in a new car. Instead of jumping on the information, especially since his notes indicated that the wife's parents had been uncooperative, he decided to put it on his desk for tomorrow. Well, tomorrow came and he found that the wife had left the city the night before — a lesson learned. We are going to make mistakes. I do, and you will, too. And we know that each time we do, we are less likely to stumble again.

I think that the most valuable lesson I have learned over the years is that "someone out there knows something that I should know." If any of you who have read this manual have a story to tell, you will have an avid listener if you want to write me in care of my publisher.

Tom Stelter
P.E.S.I.
P.O. Box 1428
Eau Claire, WI 54702

If you have made it to this final line without flipping through the pages, I THANK YOU!